Cosy Poems

Other books available from Macmillan Children's Books

She is Fierce: Brave, bold and beautiful poems by women
Chosen by Ana Sampson

Poems to Live Your Life By
Chosen and illustrated by Chris Riddell

A Poet for Every Day of the Year
Edited by Allie Esiri

Chosen by Gaby Morgan

Cosy Poems

MACMILLAN CHILDREN'S BOOKS

Published 2024 by Macmillan Children's Books
an imprint of Pan Macmillan
The Smithson, 6 Briset Street, London EC1M 5NR
EU representative: Macmillan Publishers Ireland Ltd, 1st Floor,
The Liffey Trust Centre, 117–126 Sheriff Street Upper
Dublin 1, D01 YC43
Associated companies throughout the world
www.panmacmillan.com

ISBN 978-1-0350-4867-0

Copyright © Macmillan Children's Books 2024

The right of Gaby Morgan to be identified as the
compiler of this work has been asserted by her
in accordance with the Copyright, Designs and Patents Act 1988.

The permissions acknowledgements on pages 192–194 constitute
an extension of this copyright page.

All rights reserved. No part of this publication may be reproduced,
stored in a retrieval system, or transmitted, in any form or by any means
(electronic, mechanical, photocopying, recording or otherwise),
without the prior written permission of the publisher.

Pan Macmillan does not have any control over, or any responsibility for,
any author or third-party websites referred to in or on this book.

1 3 5 7 9 8 6 4 2

A CIP catalogue record for this book is available from the British Library.

Printed and bound by CPI Group (UK) Ltd, Croydon CR0 4YY

This book is sold subject to the condition that it shall not, by way of trade or otherwise,
be lent, resold, hired out, or otherwise circulated without the publisher's prior consent in
any form of binding or cover other than that in which it is published and without a similar
condition including this condition being imposed on the subsequent purchaser.

For Grant, Jude and Evie –
I hear it in the deep heart's core
xx

Contents

A Summer Morning	*Rachel Field*	1
Three Good Things	*Jan Dean*	2
Leisure	*W. H. Davies*	3
12 good things to do where I live	*Pie Corbett*	4
Wild Garlic	*Dom Conlon*	6
First Run of Spring	*Nicola Davies*	7
Gazelle	*Steven Camden*	8
Free	*Kate Wakeling*	10
Let No One Steal Your Dreams	*Paul Cookson*	12
Joy at the Sound	*Roger McGough*	13
Things People Have Told Me in the Past Few Weeks	*Shauna Darling Robertson*	14
Friendship	*Dinah Maria Craik*	15
Friend	*Laura Mucha*	16
The Strawberry-Yogurt Smell of Words	*Mandy Coe*	17
New Friends and Old Friends	*Joseph Parry*	18
Reminder on Friendship	*Nikita Gill*	19
Laughter	*Dawn McLachlan*	20
The Human Touch	*Spencer Michael Free*	21
One Voice	*John Dougherty*	22
See a Wish	*Julie Stevens*	23

Small Wonders	*Brian Patten*	24
I Felt Wonder	*Andrea Shavick*	25
The Magic of the Brain	*Jenny Joseph*	26
It is Eternity Now ...	*Pie Corbett*	28
And So I Write	*Joshua Seigal*	29
Twinkle Twinkle	*Nicola Davies*	30
Give Yourself a Hug	*Grace Nichols*	31
Hug	*Rhiannon Oliver*	32
Hug	*Neal Zetter*	33
Winter	*Tony Bradman*	34
Home	*James Carter*	35
Hygge	*Nick Toczek*	36
What Makes Home ...?	*Jane Newberry*	37
Home	*Elena de Roo*	38
What Cosy Is	*Nick Toczek*	39
Cosy	*Anna Wilson*	40
If We Have More Words for Good Things, Do We Feel Better?	*Shauna Darling Robertson*	43
Cosy	*Michaela Morgan*	45
What is Cosy?	*Michaela Morgan*	46
Triolet in Praise of Contrast	*Rachel Piercey*	47
A Recipe for Cosiness	*Rhiannon Oliver*	48
Hot Chocolate	*Imogen Russell Williams*	49
Hot Chocolate	*Roger Stevens*	51
Hot Chocolate	*Rashmi Sirdeshpande*	52

Sam Asks Alexa About Wellbeing	Shauna Darling Robertson	53
Gran's Unknitting	Sue Hardy Dawson	55
Knit Two Together	Celia Warren	57
Recreation	Elma Mitchell	58
New Dad at Dawn	Matt Abbott	60
The Little Bottle of Silence	Chrissie Gittins	63
Pockets	Ruth Awolola	64
The Music I Like	Ian McMillan	65
Magic Hour at the Kitchen Disco	Rhiannon Oliver	66
Into the West	Nicola Davies	67
Driving at Night with My Dad	John Rice	68
Between You, Me and the Moon	Dom Conlon	70
Invitation to Love	Paul Laurence Dunbar	71
Camomile Tea	Katherine Mansfield	72
Sunset	D. H. Lawrence	73
The Power of Quiet	Emma Perry	74
Blanket Song	Rachel Piercey	75
Lullaby	Elena de Roo	77
I Am the Lullaby	Lindsay MacRae	78
Nest	Imogen Russell Williams	79
At the Fireside	Shauna Darling Robertson	81

Quietly Remarkable	*Dom Conlon*	82
Mrs Everest	*Chrissie Gittins*	84
The Blink of a Mountain	*A. F. Harrold*	85
Small Things	*Ruth Awolola*	86
May You Always	*Paul Cookson*	87
Happiness	*Sue Hardy Dawson*	88
A Reminder	*Shauna Darling Robertson*	89
My Head is Full of Hurry	*Laura Mucha*	90
In 150 Characters or Less	*Nikita Gill*	91
Don't Quit	*Traditional*	92
New Every Morning	*Susan Coolidge*	93
from The Book of Ecclesiastes		94
Desiderata	*Max Ehrmann*	95
High Flight	*John Gillespie Magee Jr.*	98
Courage	*Amelia Earhart*	99
Freedom	*Olive Runner*	100
The Train in the Night	*A. F. Harrold*	101
from Give Me the Splendid Silent Sun	*Walt Whitman*	102
Three Autumn Haikus	*Emma Perry*	103
Bonfire Stars	*Karl Newson*	104
Digging	*Edward Thomas*	105
Suffolk Hare	*Chrissie Gittins*	106
Autumn Gilt	*Valerie Bloom*	107
I Set Out to Seek the Truth	*Pie Corbett*	108

The Song of Wandering Aengus	W. B. Yeats	111
Moonlit Apples	John Drinkwater	112
To Autumn	John Keats	113
Autumn Fires	Robert Louis Stevenson	115
The Garden in September	Robert Bridges	116
Remember, Remember	Dawn McLachlan	118
Pleasant Scents	Wes Magee	119
Sonnet Moon	Debra Bertulis	120
On the First Frost of Winter	Nikita Gill	121
Raised in Rhyme	Nicola Davies	122
A Good Book	Rachel Piercey	124
Poetry	Liz Brownlee	125
This Poem . . .	Elma Mitchell	126
Between the Covers	A. F. Harrold	127
The Lake Isle of Innisfree	W. B. Yeats	128
The Promenade of Whitley Bay	Matt Abbott	129
Pangur Bán	Anon.	131
Refuge	Imogen Russell Williams	133
Rainy Day at the Caravan	Sarah Ziman	134
Mr McGuire	Brian Patten	136
Love	J. H. Rice	137
Happy	Sue Cowling	138

The Shape of a Good Greyhound	Anon.	139
from The Winter Morning Walk	William Cowper	140
Dog	Harold Monro	141
The Now Dog	Mark Bird	143
How to Work like a Dog	Imogen Russell Williams	144
Judy's on the Case	Roger Stevens	145
On ',,,;;pppppp'[[[[[[[[[[[[;'; ////////////////////////3,'	Brian Bilston	146
The Queen	Naomi Jones	148
Happiness Motor	Mandy Coe	149
Applause	Kit Wright	150
from Jubilate Agno	Christopher Smart	151
and a tree	Kate Wakeling	155
The Copper Beech at Fagervik	Laura Mucha	157
Pied Beauty	Gerard Manley Hopkins	158
The Glory	Edward Thomas	159
from To General Hamley	Alfred, Lord Tennyson	160
On the Sussex Downs	Sara Teasdale	161
Who Goes Where?	Nicola Davies	162
Crowds of Clouds	A. F. Harrold	163
Careless Rambles	John Clare	165
Two Haikus	Graham Denton	166

On the First Leaves of Autumn	*Nikita Gill*	167
Out at Sea	*Matt Abbott*	168
The Hut by the Sea	*Ethelwyn Wetherald*	170
The Little Hill	*Mary Webb*	171
Something Told the Wild Geese	*Rachel Field*	172
Pleasant Sounds	*John Clare*	173
The Lane	*Edward Thomas*	174
Some Other Names for Rain	*Kate Wakeling*	175
Tent	*Jan Dean*	176
Trips to the Seaside	*Matt Abbott*	177
Index of First Lines		183
Index of Authors and Translators		189
Acknowledgements		192

A Summer Morning

I saw dawn creep across the sky,
And all the gulls go flying by.
I saw the sea put on its dress
Of blue mid-summer loveliness,
And heard the trees begin to stir
Green arms of pine and juniper.
I heard the wind call out and say:
'Get up, my dear, it is today.'

Rachel Field

Three Good Things

At day's end I remember
three good things.

Apples maybe – their skinshine smell
and soft froth of juice.

Water maybe – the pond in the park
dark and full of secret fish.

A mountain maybe – that I saw in a film,
or climbed last holiday,
and suddenly today it thundered up
into a playground game.
Or else an owl – I heard an owl today,
and I made bread.
My head is full of all these things,
it's hard to choose just three.

I let remembering fill me up
with all good things
so that good things will overflow
into my sleeping self,
and in the morning
good things will be waiting
when I wake.

Jan Dean

Leisure

What is this life if, full of care,
We have no time to stand and stare?

No time to stand beneath the boughs
And stare as long as sheep or cows.

No time to see, when woods we pass,
Where squirrels hide their nuts in grass.

No time to see, in broad daylight,
Streams full of stars, like skies at night.

No time to turn at Beauty's glance,
And watch her feet, how they can dance.

No time to wait till her mouth can
Enrich that smile her eyes began.

A poor life this is if, full of care,
We have no time to stand and stare.

W. H. Davies

12 good things to do where I live

You can watch red kites fly over Minchinhampton common,
catch a glimpse of golden-crested wrens and pigeons
    roost at dusk.
You can skim stones on the Stroud canal,
swing over on the rope-swing at Chalford but don't fall in,
    it's deep.
You can buy Winstone's ice cream in a cone
from the van parked near Amberley and eat frozen stars.
You can visit the farmers' market on Saturday
and buy doughnuts, frosted with icing.
You can swim on a hot day at Stratford Park and splash
    sunlight.
You can cross the River Severn
and look for wild boar in the Forest of Dean.
You can stand in Selsey church and watch the sunlight glow
through the stained-glass windows,
casting rainbow shadows and feel the cool of stone.

You can buy fresh, warm bread from Hobbs House Bakery
and eat it warm with a hot sausage roll.
You can hit the cycle track and speed along the canal.
You can go to the cinema, eat popcorn,
slurp lemonade and then go upstairs to the bowling alley.
You can watch the sun slip over the distant hills like a
   great red coin.
You can stand in Farm Lane where there are no lights at
   night
and wait for the badgers that rootle for worms
and crunch snails like boiled sweets
beneath an orange harvest moon.

Pie Corbett

Wild Garlic

We were walking in the woods
after the rain
you and I two notes in search
of a new tune
when the river's strings
sang its green song out of the ground
like onions growing out of cellos
at 4a.m.

Wild garlic sang the chorus
as we breathed the melody
only the recently bereaved can hear
and I told you we'd make pesto and pasta
and your mouth began to dance
back into a smile and suddenly
I knew the words which could
break a silence at 4a.m.
turn our tears into semi-quavers
a solo into a duet.

Hurry, gather as much as you can.
Tomorrow it will flower.

Dom Conlon

First Run of Spring

In the lanes there is still a negotiation with ice
and snow drifts hang through the hedges
like Winter's big, white bum.
But the Sky is bird coloured:
bruised mauve of wood pigeon,
peach of chaffinch with wild streaks of bullfinch,
and the air sings dawn, dawn, dawn
down to every capillary and cell,
until my body rings.

Nicola Davies

Gazelle

Staring out of the window again
the green of the pitches is calling again
feel that itch in my muscles, the sigh in my bones
as the teacher's voice muffles, I drift on my own
breathe in, close my eyes
breathe out and I'm there
outside on the grass, surrounded by air
No talking, no questions, no turn of the screw
just the drum in my heart telling me what to do
so I
run
and I run
and I run and I run
and the faster I go
the more I become
I am bullet and arrow
and cheetah
gazelle
I am peregrine falcon and phoenix from hell
I am synapse and fibre and neuron
and flame
I am Thor's hammer lightning, too cosmic to tame
I am me
when I run
I can see
when I run
there is nothing that I cannot be when I run
I am anything
everything
cutting through time
And yet somehow

I'm completely
still in my mind
when I

run

can I

run

let me

run

long to

run

have to

run

and just

run

and just
run

and just

Steven Camden

Free

and we will open all the doors
and we will jump on all the beds
and we will leap from mountain top to mountain top
and we will laugh until we think we might explode
and we will laugh especially in those moments when we aren't really supposed to
and we will of course find this only makes the laughing a million times more extreme
and we will talk to animals
and we will stride across oceans
and we will dance like maniacs
and we will lie on the sofa watching TV with our shoes on because why not
and we will have long baths/short baths/no baths delete as applicable
and we will eat delicious foods
and we will not eat any of the bits we don't really like
and we will talk while lying on our backs and looking at the sky

and we will say the first thing that pops into our heads
and we will be always with our friends even when we
    are not
and we will smile with smiles so deep they make our
    eyes disappear
and we will grow wings
and we will
and we will
and we will

Kate Wakeling

Let No One Steal Your Dreams

Let no one steal your dreams
Let no one tear apart
The burning of ambition
That fires the drive inside your heart

Let no one steal your dreams
Let no one tell you that you can't
Let no one hold you back
Let no one tell you that you won't

Set your sights and keep them fixed
Set your sights on high
Let no-one steal your dreams
Your only limit is the sky

Let no one steal your dreams
Follow your heart, follow your soul
For only when you follow them
Will you feel truly whole

Set your sights and keep them fixed
Set your sights on high
Let no one steal your dreams
Your only limit is the sky

Paul Cookson

Joy at the Sound

Joy at the silver birch fluffing its leaves
Joy at the bounce of the wagtail's tail

Joy at the swirl of cold milk in the blue bowl
Joy at the blink of its bubbles

Joy at the cat revving up on the lawn
Joy at the frogs that leapfrog to freedom

Joy at the screen that fizzes to life
Joy at The Simpsons, Lisa and Bart

Joy at the dentist: 'Fine, see you next year'
Joy at the school gates: 'Closed'

Joy at the sound of children at play
Joy at the bell at the end of the day

Joy at the silver withholding the chocolate
Joy at the poem, two verses to go

Joy at the zing of the strings of the racquet
Joy at the ping of the bright yellow ball

Joy at the key unlocking the door
Joy at the sound of your voice in the hall.

Roger McGough

Things People Have Told Me in the Past Few Weeks

You need a strong core to excel at rock climbing.
If I go to Edinburgh, I'll have a blast.
We can be short-sighted and long-sighted, both at the same time.
As an actor, Michael Cera has often been typecast.
    Most of our communications have moved online.

There are so many things that need to be assessed
when you're choosing a new wheelchair.
In English, there are more than forty ways to say 'yes'.
I really ought to listen to Lily Allen's *Not Fair*.
    Young people suffer from higher rates of loneliness.

My new blue shirt looks really great.
In Yiddish, a grumbly person is called a kvetch.
The West has let down Afghanistan in so many ways.
Bolivia's top two languages are Spanish and Quechua.
    Most people don't really know what to say.

When people feel seen and heard, given the time of day,
they're far more likely to rise, to shine.
The first writing media were tablets made of clay.
Here's a conversation starter: 'I feel lonely sometimes.
    Do you ever feel that way?'

Shauna Darling Robertson

Friendship

Oh, the comfort –
the inexpressible comfort of feeling *safe* with a person –
having neither to weigh thoughts nor measure words,
but pouring them all right out,
just as they are,
chaff and grain together;
certain that a faithful hand will take and sift them,
keep what is worth keeping,
and then with the breath of kindness blow the rest away.

Dinah Maria Craik

Friend

when   I am
empty but full
of echoes, you find
me, uncrumple me
and cloak me in
kindness
thank
you

Laura Mucha

The Strawberry-Yogurt Smell of Words

Once we made a telephone
– string, stretched between two yogurt pots.
'Hello? Hello?'
Communication!
You spoke. I heard.

It's a solitary game now,
the thumb-dance of text, beep of fax,
but I still recall the buzz of string,
the strawberry-yogurt
smell of words.

Mandy Coe

New Friends and Old Friends

Make new friends, but keep the old;
Those are silver, these are gold.
New-made friendships, like new wine,
Age will mellow and refine.
Friendships that have stood the test –
Time and change – are surely best;
Brow may wrinkle, hair grow grey,
Friendship never knows decay.
For 'mid old friends, tried and true,
Once more we our youth renew.
But old friends, alas! may die,
New friends must their place supply.
Cherish friendship in your breast –
New is good, but old is best;
Make new friends, but keep the old;
Those are silver, these are gold.

Joseph Parry

Reminder on Friendship

Some friends are temporary,
Not because you hurt them
Or they hurt you.

But because friendships
Are like seasons sometimes.

Outgrowing a friend may hurt
But it's something you must do.

Every meadow
must let go of its flowers in winter,
so it can grow fresh ones in spring.

Nikita Gill

Laughter

I don't care if the winter comes
Because in your laugh you bring the sun
When you laugh the summer rolls
And I can bask in a glow that fills my soul
And lifts me higher
    than the sky and I
        am swept away
In the remembering I am warmed again
By the fondness of thinking of you
    my dear friend
In the darkest months there is always light
And there you are, dazzling bright
And you lift me higher
    than the sky and I
        am swept away
Together we can fight the sadness
    and the storms
Because I've grown so used to feeling warm

Dawn McLachlan

The Human Touch

'Tis the human touch in this world that counts,
    The touch of your hand and mine,
Which means far more to the fainting heart
    Than shelter and bread and wine;
For shelter is gone when the night is o'er,
    And bread lasts only a day.
But the touch of the hand and the sound of the voice
    Sing on in the soul alway.

Spencer Michael Free

One Voice

One voice
Rippling in the darkness like moonlight on silver water
Is joined by another: deep, resonant
Warm like the earth on a summer's day
Then a third, harmonies dancing high like a small bird
And the lights brighten, and the voices grow
Until
Surrounded by sound, enfolded in music
My own voice awakens
And I feel the song fill me.

John Dougherty

See a Wish

Bring me the sail of your breath
carry it to me and
put it in here.
I need the rumble of music
the first drop of rain
your morning words.

Bring me the edge of a wing
the back of a cloud
the top of a flake.
I need the sigh of a snail
the tremble of a fly
the drift of sand.

Bring me the sway of leaves
the pain of a splinter
the strength of a wave.
I need the call of an owl
the end of a tunnel
the jewel of water.

Bring me a silky tear
a lucky thought
a puff of smoke.
Bring me rays
bring me storms
bring me hush.

Carry them to me and
put them in here,
I can make anything happen.

Julie Stevens

Small Wonders

Brand-new elephants roamed through the jungles.
Brand-new whales splashed down through the
        oceans.
God had slapped them together,
As happy as a kid making mud pies.
He wiped His hands clean. 'Now for the hard part,'
        He thought.
He took his workbench into the garden.
Delicately He placed in the bee's sting,
The moth's antenna.
Into the salmon he placed
The memory of rivers,
His hand, not trembling in the slightest.

Brian Patten

I Felt Wonder

I felt wonder
witnessing a total eclipse of the sun,
the first time I saw falling snow,
the time when I stuck my finger to a glacier,
and hopping over steaming embers inside a volcano

I felt wonder
collecting my new kitten from the rehoming centre,
tasting my first home-grown tomato,
making jam that was actually edible,
discovering a Beethoven concerto

I felt overwhelming wonder when I held my newborn
    babies
and now, when I hold my gorgeous grandbabies
and when I realise I've lived all my life through peacetime

but then I began to think, that's it for wonders . . .
there can't be anything else for me so gloriously new
but I have lately been surprised at yet another wonder
because I asked the world for happiness,
and then I met you

Andrea Shavick

The Magic of the Brain

Such a sight I saw:
An eight-sided kite surging up into a cloud
Its eight tails streaming out as if they were one.
It lifted my heart as starlight lifts the head
Such a sight I saw.

And such a sound I heard.
One bird through dim winter light as the day was closing
Poured out a song suddenly from an empty tree.
It cleared my head as water refreshes the skin
Such a sound I heard.

Such a smell I smelled:
A mixture of roses and coffee, of green leaf and warmth.
It took me to gardens and summer and cities abroad,
Memories of meetings as if my past friends were here
Such a smell I smelled.

Such soft fur I felt:
It wrapped me around, soothing my winter-cracked skin,
Not gritty or stringy or sweaty but silkily warm
As my animal slept on my lap, and we both breathed
    content
Such soft fur I felt.

Such food I tasted:
Smooth-on-tongue soup, and juicy crackling of meat,
Greens like fresh fields, sweet-on-your-palate peas,
Jellies and puddings with fragrance of fruit they are
    made from
Such good food I tasted.

Such a world comes in:
Far world of the sky to breathe in through your nose
Near world you feel underfoot as you walk on the land.
Through your eyes and your ears and your mouth and
    your brilliant brain –
Such a world comes in.

Jenny Joseph

It is Eternity Now . . .

It is eternity now. I am in the midst of it. It is about me in the sunshine; I am in it, as the butterfly floats in the light-laden air. Nothing has to come; it is now. Now is eternity; now is the immortal life.

Richard Jefferies, The Story of my Heart (1883)

as the butterfly floats in the light-laden air,
as the sun sifts through thin cloud in the golden valley,
as the taxis queue at the early morning station,
as the spider's web clings to the gatepost,
as the postman's van climbs Farm Lane,
as the school children wait on the corner for the school bus,
as the bees begin their business amongst the lavender,
as the coffee machine gargles,
as the radio clears its throat,
as the grey cat stalks across our garden unaware of trespass,
as the buddleia waits for the first tortoiseshell,
as the post slips onto the carpet,
as the day begins,
it is now,
as we move through eternity,
as we savour and sip each waking moment,
of this one unremarkable,
remarkable life.

Pie Corbett

And So I Write

the word LOVE in my diary, to remind myself
of the underpinning of all the things I do.
I craft the letters with a ruler,

taking great pains to ensure that everything
is smooth, straight, in order. I decorate the word
with a border and I colour it all in, in a way

I haven't done since primary school.
I really want this word to stand out – LOVE.
The unassailable axiom; the uncaused cause;

that than which nothing greater can be conceived.
Until I realise that the letters aren't quite even.
Some of the lines are thicker than others

and if you squint a bit you can see
a slight smudge on the page. The letter O
seems sort of squished, and although the word

is still, recognisably, LOVE, it looks somewhat
misformed, somehow. And so I carry now
this buckled LOVE everywhere I go –

in my diary, tucked tight in my rucksack –
and this imperfection is part of everything I do,
a bold, flawed LOVE on the pages of my days.

Joshua Seigal

Twinkle Twinkle

Close the door and turn the key
We're alone now you and me.

Slowly we will climb the stairs
Leave below our woes and cares

Close as silver spoons we'll lie
While the moon sails in the sky.

Trouble will rise with the day,
For now, just hold me close and say

'Twinkle twinkle little star,
How I wonder what you are!'

Nicola Davies

Give Yourself a Hug

Give yourself a hug
when you feel unloved

Give yourself a hug
when people put on airs
to make you feel a bug

Give yourself a hug
when everyone seems to give you
a cold-shoulder shrug

Give yourself a hug –
a big big hug

And keep on singing,
'Only one in a million like me
Only one in a million-billion-thrillion-zillion
like me.'

Grace Nichols

Hug

Snug as a bug in a duvet-thick rug
Safe as a house full of dreams
Smooth as a stone that swirls to the sea,
Polished by sinuous streams.

Soft as a purr, soft as kittenish fur
Strong as sunbeams that displace the night
Sure as the wind blows, this one thing I know:
Your hug can make everything right.

Rhiannon Oliver

Hug

Give me a hug
With warm wraparound arms
Give me a hug
Cosy, cuddly, calm

Give me a hug
So I know that you care
Give me a hug
Like a grizzly bear

Give me a hug
Your great miracle cure
Give me a hug
It's what real friends are for

Give me a hug
Make it tender and tight
Give me a hug
Anytime day or night

Give me a hug
When my spirits are low
Give me a hug
And please – never let go

Neal Zetter

Winter

It's warm by our fire,
It's cosy and nice;
My feet in their slippers
Like two winter mice.

A drink and a biscuit,
A cuddle with Dad,
A book before bedtime –
And I won't be bad.

Time for some TV,
Time for some hugs,
I'm snug as a mouse
Or a bug in a rug.

I don't mind the winter,
I don't mind the cold –
At least when I'm home
With a hot drink to hold!

Tony Bradman

Home

It's not the bricks
that build the walls
nor what's behind
the many doors

It's anytime
it's anywhere
a space within
this world we share

From where we roam
to where we live
to where we chill
to whom we're with

Our one unique
and precious place
where we're ourselves
our souls feel safe

Perhaps a book,
a view, a chair,
or maybe time
away somewhere

A crowded room
or just alone
we all deserve
and need that home

James Carter

Hygge
(pronounced who-gu)

Well, I guess you've never heard
of this very special word
which has flown, just like a bird,
from Danish into English
to nest here in our language.

It's a mood, a place, a feeling
of true comfort, warmth and healing
like four walls, a floor, a ceiling
far from fear which wars are dealing
or what poverty's been stealing.

So that's sorted. Now you've heard
of this special migrant word
which, like refugee or bird,
will settle here in English,
be comfy, free from anguish,
made welcome in our language.

Nick Toczek

What Makes Home . . . ?

I ask, and from the depths
of the saggy sofa they shout
buttered toast! and I scoff derisively
and say toast is merely bread charred with love
and more tea brews in the brown pot
while little pops and hisses spring from the fire.

Home is all the bring-home laundry
done in the night by the fairies.
Home is never running out of teabags
or playing a board game by the fireside
that I can never hope to win.
Home is a fridge decked with toddler art.

Home means peace and night owls;
a happy dog breaking the rules
over and over. Home is the scent of
lemon geraniums by the back door,
snuggly blankets, proper baskets
and a *real* bear-hug on the doorstep.

Jane Newberry

Home

House

Hut

Boat

Bus

A tent beneath the stars

A tribe

Or just the two of us

We know it, when we are

Elena de Roo

What Cosy Is

Cosy is comfort and cosy is snug.
Cosy's so warm you don't care, you just shrug.
Cosy's the den that you've secretly dug.
Cosy protects you from threat and from thug.

Cosy embraces you in its safe hug.
Cosy's your inglenook, jacket and rug.
Cosy turns fever and fright to humbug.
Cosy cures all. It's your miracle drug.

Cosy is kindly. Its smile's never smug.
Cosy calls your name with welcoming tug.
Cosy's this precious place we poets plug.
Cosy's the soup that you sip from life's mug.

Nick Toczek

Cosy

Such a small word
for such a big feeling.

A big, warm, snuggly feeling
which spreads through you
like a drink of hot chocolate
filling you up
on a cold winter's day.
Or a huge, fluffy, woolly blanket
You can use to make yourself
into a giant, comfy person-parcel.

Not all languages have a word for 'cosy'.
Some borrow it, as the French do.
'C'est cosy!' they say,
as they cuddle up in a warm café
and look out at the streets
on a crisp, sunny, Paris Sunday.

Other languages have similar words.
The Danes say, '*hygge*' –
a lovely, friendly word that looks like a hug
and means something like cosy,
but also: safe, comfy
or being happy
with the ones that you love.

The Dutch say, '*Gezelligheid*' –
a bouncy, happy, smiley word
which means you're completely at ease,
relaxed
and enjoying yourself
with the people you care about.

The Japanese say, '*ikigai*' –
a gentle, thoughtful word
which is almost a philosophy,
a way of living
which encourages you
to do what you are good at,
and do it well
in the best way that you can
so that your life becomes more meaningful.

But none of these words are the same as 'cosy' –
not exactly.
None of them conjure up that feeling you have
When you let your cat
nestle into your lap
or your dog
curls up at your feet
while the lights are turned down low
and the fire crackles in the grate
and the smell of hot buttered toast
wafts into the room
while you put your hands around a hot mug
of tomato soup
and hold it to your chest
so the steam warms your face
as you smile at the snow
falling thick and soft
on the ground outside your window.

That's cosy.

Such a small word
for such a big feeling.

Anna Wilson

If We Have More Words for Good Things, Do We Feel Better?

I heard there's a word in Bantu
for the irresistible urge to shed your clothes
while dancing   *Mbuki-mvuki*

In Dutch you need just one word to say
when I go outside and walk in the wind
I come alive   *Uitwaaien*

Norwegians enjoying
a cold drink outside on a hot day
can sum up that feeling with a word   *Utepils*

In the Philippines, a single word captures
that fizzy feeling you get
when you're talking to someone you fancy   *Kilig*

Germans can relax with a word that says
I feel protected
and safe from harm   *Geborgenheit*

In Hebrew there's a word
for sauntering, carefree
down a particular street in Tel Aviv   *Lehizdangef*

Swedes can name
the gentle, welcoming space
between two embracing arms *Famn*

And in English (go figure)
we have a word for this:
the overwhelming desire to kiss *Basorexia*

Shauna Darling Robertson

Cosy

Rain dripping at the window,
and I'm in bed.

Wind whooshing at the window,
and I'm home in bed.

Snow falling in the distance.
I'm here in my snug bed.

Hail tippy tapping,
Snow gently falling,
Wind wildly whooshing,
Rain slowly dripping,
and I'm curled up, with a book, in my warm bed.

Outside the world
and all of its weather.
In here my blanket up to my nose.
My nose in a book.
My books all around.
Around me my blanket, my familiar toys.
My toes are toasty, there's a warm drink waiting.
Sounds of radio and humming from downstairs
Me in my warm bed.
Cosy.

Michaela Morgan

What is Cosy?

Cosy is ...
As cuddly warm as the softest scarf.
As happy as the biggest smile – or the loudest laugh.
As soothing as a bowl of your favourite soup or food.
As cheering as your friend who calls, when you're in a sad and grumpy mood.
As hopeful as the fairy lights on a grim grey winter day.
Cosy is ...
simply the warmest and the safest feeling.
OK?

Michaela Morgan

Triolet in Praise of Contrast

Oh, warmth is sweeter after cold
and dry is warmer after rain.
For contrast makes our senses bold,
so warmth is sweeter after cold,
while greyness makes the lamplight gold,
and wildness at the window pane
says *Warmth is sweeter after cold*
and dry is warmer after rain.

Rachel Piercey

A Recipe for Cosiness

First, take a rain shower and run through it
Find a puddle and dip your feet (repeat until socks are
    soaked)
Ensure raindrops drip from your nose, your lashes

When you have fully drenched yourself in the day
Let the water shiver briefly on your skin
Retreat indoors

Run a bath as hot as your elbows can bear
Pour in bubbles (aim for thick cappuccino -like foam)
Soak for twenty minutes
Dry with silk-soft towel and dress in oversized pyjamas

Mix steaming milk, chocolate, marshmallows
(Allow time for marshmallows to reach for each other)
Close curtains, dim lights, sprinkle cushions and hope

Wrap yourself in a warm blanket and open book
Breathe in the scent of safety
Keep hot chocolate close

Leave to rest for at least an hour and enjoy

Rhiannon Oliver

Hot Chocolate

Wet denim clings like concrete.
A line of mudprints trails me up the path:
bad luck, grim sludge, deep gloom.

That sneaky sun, stealing
from warmth and brightness into damp grey mist –
then god-size belly rumbles

and a *cloudburst*.

Now look at me:
rain plipping tepid from my rat-tailed hair,
my favourite trainers ruined.

Sodden fabric
plasters my cold-bumped skin. The dark hall smells:
old sweat, damp feet, fresh misery.

Then a silhouette
of Dad stands in the kitchen's steamy light.
Behind him, on the stove, the milk

just simmers.

Pizza cremator,
notorious combustor of baked spuds –
hot chocolate magician.

As he grates milk and dark,
whisks up a frothy storm, stirs in a pinch
of cinnamon, and pours,

I feel
the cold lift from my bones, my dread give way
to shivers of contentment;

and as my hands close
round the hot mug swirled high with squirty cream
it's like the sun comes out:

in lamplight,
curling steam, stove burner, open fridge
and on both faces

broad, cream-bearded smiles.

Imogen Russell Williams

Hot Chocolate

The waiter
places the cup before me
and smiles

I turn it slightly
to align the handle
at 90 degrees

I lean forward
breath in the milky
chocolate aroma

Gaze at the foam
settling on the surface
slow my thoughts

My phone
hums
I'll be there in five

I wrap my cold hands
around the hot cup
and lift it to my lips

Roger Stevens

Hot Chocolate

As the rain thunders
against the window,
freezing fingertips
curl around
hot mugs of cocoa.

Sip, sigh, smile, repeat.
And somehow, slowly,
everything begins to feel
so much better.

Rashmi Sirdeshpande

Sam Asks Alexa About Wellbeing

after George Szirtes

What is wellbeing, asks Sam. It starts with freedom, says Alexa, which spins around until it feels dizzy and then has a little lie down.

What is wellbeing, asks Sam. A giant slice of cake that's hearteningly solid and as light and fluffy as air, says Alexa.

What is wellbeing, asks Sam. A cross between a pillow, a pair of skis and a lioness, says Alexa.

What is wellbeing, asks Sam. A house that can fly, says Alexa.

What is wellbeing, asks Sam. I'm not sure but I think it might be a deep green, says Alexa.

What is wellbeing, asks Sam. A kind of hologram, says Alexa. Imagine looking into the cells of an orange and seeing the whole orange and also every other fruit in there.

What is wellbeing, asks Sam. A rocking chair that's also a rope ladder to the stars, says Alexa.

What is wellbeing, asks Sam. Pages of a book talking and laughing about the times they had when they were trees, says Alexa.

What is wellbeing, asks Sam. The heart and the mind and the world on the same page, says Alexa, or thereabouts.

Shauna Darling Robertson

Gran's Unknitting

Gran pulls out yellow wool
she holds the sun
scraps of late summer
from worn cardigans
her eyes close –

slowly unknitting them
she hums
a rainbow resting on her thumbs
a bluebell jersey shrinks
to wood and stream
and from old gloves
fall shades of autumn leaves

each thread unfolds
its wriggled release
she pulls out twigs
unravels cobweb sleeves
their stiches dropped
empty buttons grin.

I dream of sheep
swallowing sunlight
rain from heather
plaid fields
gorse and lichen

fleeces of buttercup
and celandine
sheep unpicking river-
meadow and hill
knitting new lambs
whilst the world lies still . . .

Sue Hardy Dawson

Knit Two Together

for Granny & Granddad

She sits and knits,
yarn spinning yarn,
while he nods and whispers,
pen in hand

and she knits 10 Across
into her row,
stitching them together,
strand by strand

till all they know
and all they ever did,
fit like letters
in the crossword grid.

Celia Warren

Recreation

She makes embroidery
As bees make honey
From flowers and colours.

It absorbs her.
She is drawn by threads
Into the heart of the pattern.

In the slipping, bitty
Ripples of domesticity
She likes the sedentary

Intricate necessity
Of this embroidery.
It must be just so, exactly,

And yet can wait, not spoiling,
Not boiling over, when
She lays it down (for cries

Of children, phone, kettle).
She rises, goes
To do whatever she has to

And returns to the quiet tugging
Of thread, unbroken,
Piecing together (when she has a moment)

Complete, unwithering roses.

Elma Mitchell

New Dad at Dawn

The box tumbles open
on the mustard rug.
Wooden shapes in primary colours:
20 of them scattered.

And the lamp's on,
by the bookcase,
because daylight's only creeping.
And I marvel
as his tiny fingers
align
and rotate.

He is 16 months old
and I am smitten.

He used to be terrible at this.
Properly dreadful!
Just an aimless claw:
jamming L-shape
on to four-point star.
But *now*...?
They're slotting through
at three or four per minute.

And I wonder
how long it'll be
before I won't need to guide the box.

On the TV,
he ignores the cartoons
that illuminated my childhood.
The original series
of 'Fireman Sam.'
Gerry Anderson's 'Thunderbirds.'

But who needs screens
when all these shapes
are hopelessly discarded?
And who needs sleep
past 5 a.m.
when he claps himself
and giggles.

I am so ludicrously,
fandabidozily,
overwhelmingly,
in love with him.

Just to hoist him up
for a wriggly cuddle
is the cream on any day.

I am dizzy
with tiredness
but delirious
with awe.

As his dinky arms
lift the box of shapes
and launch them
across the floor.

Matt Abbott

The Little Bottle of Silence

for Sally Crabtree

In my kitchen I have a little bottle of silence.
It's packed full of the gaps
between a duck quacking at her young,

the lull after an alarm goes off,
the hush when the kettle goes off the boil.

Folded over these moments are
the pause between lightning and thunder,
the stillness of a new puddle after a storm,

the calm after the crowd cheers,
the quiet before a firework explodes.

Finally, just under the stopper,
is the tranquillity of a June garden,
the peace of an empty road,

and the long sleep of a new born babe.

Chrissie Gittins

Pockets

Her pockets are never empty.
She says pockets are for running.
So she keeps them full,
Stuffs universes into them,
And says it is just the essentials.

She says: if we get stranded,
If aliens take us,
If there's an apocalypse,
There will be no time for bags.

She treats pockets
Like built -in spaces for hope.
Lets the weight of it
Pull down her baggy trousers.

Readies herself for any eventuality,
Revels in her own lack of normality.

Ruth Awolola

The Music I Like

The Music I like
Is very special music.

At this moment,
For instance,

I'm listening to the washing machine
Slowing down,

As the gerbil rattles
In its cage,

And my wife runs
Up the stairs

And my next-door neighbour
Cuts his grass.

Music, very special music
Just listen . . .

Ian McMillan

Magic Hour at the Kitchen Disco

There's a special light when it's nearly night

And your shoulders dip down low

When the need to *do* has passed for you

You're the mum I used to know

Songs stream in and I begin

Starting steady, slow

Then you take the chance, get up, dance

And our feet just go-go-go

We shift in time as the music climbs

Finding our own flow

And it's just you and me, you and me

And the kitchen is a-glow

Rhiannon Oliver

Into the West

Heading west, the names cwtch round
Pont and pant,
Cwm and bryn.
Every signpost is a comfort.
And the hills fold me in

Nicola Davies

Driving at Night with My Dad

Open the window,
the cool summer night swooshes in.
My favourite music playing loud.

2 a.m. – summer's midnight –
neither of us can sleep
so we go for a night drive.

Stars crowd the sky
and twinkle at us in code.
Our headlights reply in light-language.

A fox crosses, red and grey,
and arches under a fence:
rabbits run and a farm cat's eyes
catch our beam.
She stares at us for a second of stretched time . . .
. . . her eyes two new coins.

Through villages that are asleep,
past farms that are warm,
past houses that are dreaming,
under trees that are resting,
past birds that have no flight, no song.

I sense I am in some other country
where day, time, people no longer matter.
In this huge dark,
through the somewhere and the nowhere
of this uninhabited world,
I feel safe and secure
driving at night with my dad.

John Rice

Between You, Me and the Moon

It gets darker later,
now that your summer is here,
but I watch cool winds carry
dandelion embers to your hair
whilst the stars I used to sing
stay faded in the air.

We sit together less often
and tonight's moon is hard to find,
but the old campfire still recalls
your bedtime books in the theatre
of its flames, whilst the snap of wet wood
brings slammed doors to mind.

You talk of new planets
as I try to hold to the old,
and the light of birthday candles,
torches in tents, and your bike's
back light takes longer to arrive.

There's too much space and yet
not enough for all you've become.
I cannot keep you with the names
of constellations, and yet we talk
of everything between you, me
and the moon.

Dom Conlon

Invitation to Love

Come when the nights are bright with stars
Or come when the moon is mellow;
Come when the sun his golden bars
Drops on the hay-field yellow.
Come in the twilight soft and gray,
Come in the night or come in the day,
Come, O love, whene'er you may,
And you are welcome, welcome.

You are sweet, O Love, dear Love,
You are soft as the nesting dove.
Come to my heart and bring it to rest
As the bird flies home to its welcome nest.

Come when my heart is full of grief
Or when my heart is merry;
Come with the falling of the leaf
Or with the redd'ning cherry.
Come when the year's first blossom blows,
Come when the summer gleams and glows,
Come with the winter's drifting snows,
And you are welcome, welcome.

Paul Laurence Dunbar

Camomile Tea

Outside the sky is light with stars;
There's a hollow roaring from the sea.
And, alas! for the little almond flowers,
The wind is shaking the almond tree.

How little I thought, a year ago,
In the horrible cottage upon the Lee
That he and I should be sitting so
And sipping a cup of camomile tea.

Light as feathers the witches fly,
The horn of the moon is plain to see;
By a firefly under a jonquil flower
A goblin toasts a bumble-bee.

We might be fifty, we might be five,
So snug, so compact, so wise are we!
Under the kitchen-table leg
My knee is pressing against his knee.

Our shutters are shut, the fire is low,
The tap is dripping peacefully;
The saucepan shadows on the wall
Are black and round and plain to see.

Katherine Mansfield

Sunset

There is a band of dull gold in the west, and say
    what you like
again and again some god of evening leans out of it
and shares being with me, silkily
all of twilight.

D. H. Lawrence

The Power of Quiet

As she let the stillness settle,

as she let the power of quiet drift around her

she felt everything

slow

       right

              down.

As the sounds of silence dripped from the ceiling

everything

became so clear.

'This,' she whispered,

'is the power of quiet.'

Emma Perry

Blanket Song

I'm tucked up,
snuggled up,
rugged up,
cuddled up,
swaddled
and swathed,
at rest.

I'm enfolded,
enveloped,
encircled,
ensconced.
I'm thankfully,
thermally
blessed.

I'm curled up
and cushioned,
cocooned
and content.
I'm as snug
as a bug
in a rug.

I am cosy
from nose
down to
thickly socked toes,
in a blissfully
blankety
hug.

Rachel Piercey

Lullaby

The hum of the city by night

The swish of distant traffic

A murmur of voices in the next room

The muffled clink of dishes

The rumbling purr-purrr-pur-r-r-r-r of the cat on my bed

and a whispering

like gentle rain

from the rustle-rustle-rustle . . . rustle-rustle-rustle-rustle . . .
    rustle-rustle-rustle-rustle . . .
        of the trees

Elena de Roo

I Am the Lullaby

I am the footsteps in the hall
I am the hand that wipes the tears
I am the stars that pierce the dark
I am the song that soothes all fears
I am the kiss that finds the cheek
I am the air where dreams take flight
I am the story's happy end
I am the lamp left on at night.

Lindsay MacRae

Nest

slapdash
loose leaf football
(rook
magpie
twist of squirrel)

a basket globe
tight braided
(vole
weaver
harvest mouse)

old blanket
fleece
knit
patchwork

(sucked corners
sleepy baby

stroked slowly
child

still loved
long teen

held dear
the whole life through)

Imogen Russell Williams

At the Fireside

The others have long since gone to bed.
I gaze at the flames. They dance and shine
and set alight sparks inside my head.
The others have long since gone to bed
but this, by far, is my favourite time –
when others have long since gone to bed.
I gaze at the flames that dance and shine.

Shauna Darling Robertson

Quietly Remarkable

You're never first
You're sometimes last
And lessons don't
Sink in so fast.
It feels as though
Your other mates
Are quick to speak
In class debates
But you're the Moon
And that's OK
You're doing fine
You're here to stay
Quietly remarkable.

You look ahead
But nothing's clear,
Every choice
Is edged with fear.
You don't know what
You'd like to do,
The jobs you see
Don't feel quite you
But you're the Moon
And that's OK
You're doing fine
You're here to stay
Quietly remarkable.

You're doing good
When that one friend
Turns to you
In the end
And you're right there
To help them out
To show them what
The world's about
Because you see it
Through your eyes
And noone else
Can be as wise
And quietly remarkable

Cos you're the Moon
And that's OK
You're doing fine
You're here to stay
Quietly remarkable.

Dom Conlon

Mrs Everest

Mrs Everest is our headteacher,
she says we're all climbing up a peak,
some of us get there quickly,
some of us take a week.

Mrs Everest says it doesn't matter how fast or
    high we climb,
what matters is we take a stride –
as long as we are trying
her smile is wide, wide, wide.

Some of us stumble on a rock,
we need a helping hand,
there's always someone to catch us,
to make it safe to land.

Chrissie Gittins

The Blink of a Mountain

Under the green
see the world turn.

It doesn't notice you
stomping about.

It was here before
and will be here after.

You stomp for a minute,
it breathes for an age.

You can rage and shout
and spill your anger on it,

but,
it's forgotten you already,

a century has flown by
in the blink of a mountain.

You are little. It is big.
Love it as you pass through.

A. F. Harrold

Small Things

Something worth losing
The feeling of winning
Words that capture feelings
Successful all-in-one orange skin peelings
Laughing until you're wheezing
Hot drinks when it's freezing
Uninterrupted sleeping
And sibling peacekeeping
Trying and striving to make every day better
All of the things that we can do together
The layers of an inside joke
And all the other small things
That give me hope.

Ruth Awolola

May You Always

May your smile be ever present
May your skies be always blue
May your path be ever upward
May your heart be ever true

May your dreams be full to bursting
May your steps be always sure
May the fire in your soul
Blaze on for evermore

May you live to meet ambition
May you strive to pass each test
May you find the love your life deserves
May you always have the best

May your happiness be plentiful
May your regrets be few
May you always be my best friend
May you always . . . just be you

Paul Cookson

Happiness

Sometimes we wear it like a scarf
wrapped tightly against the sad.

It may be as thin as silk to the wind
light as spider webs, but it shields

prevents the kind words of friends
creeping in to spoil the effect.

Others it comes unbidden, a poem
a hand brushes ours – welcome

as a caress. These are warming –
seeds that grow. They cannot be seen

But they are strong within us
the stout armour of cruel days.

If we are wise we keep them close
count them over, tight as misers

Sue Hardy Dawson

A Reminder

Like a warning shot or a siren,
a bird's cry rises above the racket
of coffee machines and pedestrian crossings.

Somewhere between a *screech* and a *bleep*,
it pierces the rush of morning. My eyes shoot up –
a sparrowhawk, circling the Pilton Estate

and in my looking I see, as if for the first time
the green and purple hills that surround this city –
spanning all sides, pulling everything close,

gathering us up in their horizon-sized folds
as if to say, *We've got this, folks. You're sheltered; safe.*
As if all of our days were held in their grace.

Shauna Darling Robertson

My Head is Full of Hurry

so I find a patch of green
and sit.

Busy birds twitter and chunter,
chit-chattering about their day.
Flies lurk, loiter and listen,
wings shimmering till they whizz away.

Bees hum, bumble and mutter,
leaves flit, float and flutter,
and a squirrel comes out to play.

Butterflies flock in an elegant flurry,
dogs in a bustle scoot, scuttle and scurry,
and amid the hustle and rustle of the glade,
my mind's hurry f
              l
                i
                 t
              t
               e
                r
              s

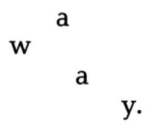

                              a
                          w
                              a
                                 y.

Laura Mucha

In 150 Characters or Less

Everything is on fire, but everyone I love is doing
    beautiful things
and trying to make life worth living,
and I know I don't have to believe in everything,
but I believe in that.

Nikita Gill

Don't Quit

When things go wrong as they sometimes will,
When the road you're trudging seems all up hill,
When the funds are low and the debts are high
And you want to smile, but you have to sigh,
When care is pressing you down a bit,
Rest if you must, but don't you quit.
Life is strange with its twists and turns
As every one of us sometimes learns
And many a failure comes about
When he might have won had he stuck it out;
Don't give up though the pace seems slow –
You may succeed with another blow.
Success is failure turned inside out –
The silver tint of the clouds of doubt,
And you never can tell just how close you are,
It may be near when it seems so far;
So stick to the fight when you're hardest hit –
It's when things seem worst that you must not quit.

Traditional

New Every Morning

Every day is a fresh beginning,
Listen my soul to the glad refrain.
And, spite of old sorrows
And older sinning,
Troubles forecasted
And possible pain,
Take heart with the day and begin again.

Susan Coolidge

from **The Book of Ecclesiastes**

To every thing there is a season,
and a time to every purpose under the heaven:
A time to be born, and a time to die;
A time to plant, and a time to pluck up that which is planted;
A time to kill, and a time to heal;
A time to break down, and a time to build up;
A time to weep, and a time to laugh;
A time to mourn, and a time to dance;
A time to cast away stones, and a time to gather stones together;
A time to embrace, and a time to refrain from embracing;
A time to get, and a time to lose;
A time to keep, and a time to cast away;
A time to rend, and a time to sew;
A time to keep silence, and a time to speak;
A time to love, and a time to hate;
A time of war, and a time of peace.

Desiderata

Go placidly amid the noise and haste,
and remember what peace there may be in silence.
As far as possible without surrender
be on good terms with all persons.
Speak your truth quietly and clearly;
and listen to others,
even the dull and the ignorant;
they too have their story.

Avoid loud and aggressive persons,
they are vexations to the spirit.
If you compare yourself with others,
you may become vain and bitter;
for always there will be greater and lesser persons
    than yourself.
Enjoy your achievements as well as your plans.

Keep interested in your own career, however humble;
it is a real possession in the changing fortunes of time.
Exercise caution in your business affairs;
for the world is full of trickery.
But let this not blind you to what virtue there is;
many persons strive for high ideals;
and everywhere life is full of heroism.

Be yourself.
Especially, do not feign affection.
Neither be cynical about love;
for in the face of all aridity and disenchantment
it is as perennial as the grass.
Take kindly the counsel of the years,
gracefully surrendering the things of youth.
Nurture strength of spirit to shield you in sudden misfortune.
But do not distress yourself with dark imaginings.
Many fears are born of fatigue and loneliness.
Beyond a wholesome discipline,
be gentle with yourself.

You are a child of the universe,
no less than the trees and the stars;
you have a right to be here.
And whether or not it is clear to you,
no doubt the universe is unfolding as it should.

Therefore be at peace with God,
whatever you conceive Him to be,
and whatever your labors and aspirations,
in the noisy confusion of life keep peace with your soul.

With all its sham, drudgery, and broken dreams,
it is still a beautiful world.
Be cheerful.
Strive to be happy.

Max Ehrmann

High Flight

Oh! I have slipped the surly bonds of earth
And danced the skies on laughter-silvered wings;
Sunward I've climbed, and joined the tumbling mirth
Of sun-split clouds—and done a hundred things
You have not dreamed of—wheeled and soared and
　swung
High in the sunlit silence. Hov'ring there
I've chased the shouting wind along, and flung
My eager craft through footless halls of air.

Up, up the long delirious, burning blue,
I've topped the windswept heights with easy grace
Where never lark, or even eagle flew—
And, while with silent lifting mind I've trod
The high unsurpassed sanctity of space,
Put out my hand and touched the face of God.

John Gillespie Magee Jr.

Courage

Courage is the price that Life exacts for granting peace.

The soul that knows it not knows no release
From little things:

Knows not the livid loneliness of fear,
Nor mountain heights where bitter joy can hear
The sound of wings.

How can life grant us boon of living, compensate
For dull gray ugliness and pregnant hate
Unless we dare

The soul's dominion? Each time we make a choice,
   we pay
With courage to behold the resistless day,
And count it fair.

Amelia Earhart

Freedom

Give me the long, straight road before me,
    A clear, cold day with a nipping air,
Tall, bare trees to run on beside me,
    A heart that is light and free from care.
Then let me go! – I care not whither
    My feet may lead, for my spirit shall be
Free as the brook that flows to the river,
    Free as the river that flows to the sea.

Olive Runner

The Train in the Night

In the pitch-like night,
as the curtains are silent,
as the stairs don't creak,
as the pipes keep mum,
as the road across town
is empty of traffic and
not even a bike bell rings,

then, across all of it,
a distant train rumbles
and grumbles and sings
and clatters across points –

the imagined lights from its windows
playing across the imagined faces
of the people who aren't waiting in their cars
at the level crossing
for it to pass –

and I roll over, listening to the thunder
knowing it's not going to rain,

that I'm hearing a train
a train
a train
a train.

A. F. Harrold

from Give Me the Splendid Silent Sun

Give me the splendid silent sun, with all his beams
    full-dazzling;
Give me juicy autumnal fruit, ripe and red from the
    orchard;
Give me a field where the unmow'd grass grows;
Give me an arbor, give me the trellis'd grape;
Give me fresh corn and wheat—give me serene-
    moving animals, teaching content;
Give me nights perfectly quiet, as on high plateaus
    west of the Mississippi, and I looking up at the stars;
Give me odorous at sunrise a garden of beautiful
    flowers, where I can walk undisturb'd;
Give me for marriage a sweet-breath'd woman, of
    whom I should never tire;
Give me a perfect child—give me, away, aside from
    the noise of the world, a rural, domestic life;
Give me to warble spontaneous songs, reliev'd, recluse
    by myself, for my own ears only;
Give me solitude—give me Nature—give me again,
    O Nature, your primal sanities!

Walt Whitman

Three Autumn Haikus

red flames flickering
beneath the endless blackness
warmth grows inside me.

wriggling niggles
awake, in the cold night air
shifting light soothes me.

the winds grip the trees
shaken from heads to their toes
leaves cascading down.

Emma Perry

Bonfire Stars

Embers swirling, twirling, whirling,
Looping, curling, glowing bright,
Dancing in the climbing sky
Towards the bonfire of the night

Karl Newson

Digging

Today I think
Only with scents, – scents dead leaves yield,
And bracken, and wild carrot's seed,
And the square mustard field;

Odours that rise
When the spade wounds the roots of tree,
Rose, currant, raspberry, or goutweed,
Rhubarb or celery;

The smoke's smell, too,
Flowing from where a bonfire burns
The dead, the waste, the dangerous,
And all to sweetness turns.

It is enough
To smell, to crumble the dark earth,
While the robin sings over again
Sad songs of Autumn mirth.

Edward Thomas

Suffolk Hare

Two church spires for ears,
amber wide-awake eyes,
you lollop towards me
as I pack the car to leave.

For a minute you fold
your unlikely legs beneath you
and we are still,
the world holds off.
Then you turn and skitter off
back down the lane.

I imagine you now gazing at the golden moon,
making sure the apples ripen,
the barley is harvested,
the fields shout with poppies and butterwort.

Chrissie Gittins

Autumn Gilt

The late September sunshine,
Lime green on the linden leaves,
Burns bronze on the slated roof-tops,
Yellow on the farmer's last sheaves.
It flares flame-like on the fire hydrant,
Is ebony on the blackbird's wing,
Blue beryl on the face of the ocean,
Glints gold on the bride's wedding ring.
A sparkling rainbow on the stained-glass window,
It's a silver sheen on the kitchen sink,
The late September sunshine
Is a chameleon, I think.

Valerie Bloom

I Set Out to Seek the Truth

Not knowing where to look,
I took the lane towards the fields
to see what time might yield . . .

as the knot grass
    moth caterpillar
        humps and bumps
           along the fence,
rests
    for a second
at the wind's touch;
its lean, stippled body
    and soft bristles ripple,

        as the whooper swan
    flexes its neck,   stretches bridal wings
  open as blank pages of frail feathers;
white washing-line sheets   take off in a flutter,
skim the lake   with a clatter,

as the orb-weaver spider
    tests each thread,
waits at the edge
    to scuttle, seize and wrap
any unsuspecting fly
    that passes by –
diamond specks of dew
    freckle the leaves;
the web clings, glittering,
    as kindly morning sun
warms the lane.

Early this morning,
while the sun set out at first light,
    I sought the truth.
Not knowing exactly
while the sun set out at first light,
    I sought the truth.
Not knowing exactly
    where to look,
I took Farm Lane
    towards the fields
to see where rambling
    might take me.

The road ahead glowed,
blackberries polka-dotted hedgerows,
blackbirds broke the silence
and clouds scudded
through sheer blue above.

Truth blossomed with every step,
every stop to stare,
and there I found
that truth
was everywhere
I chose to look.

Pie Corbett

The Song of Wandering Aengus

I went out to the hazel wood,
Because a fire was in my head,
And cut and peeled a hazel wand,
And hooked a berry to a thread;
And when white moths were on the wing,
And moth-like stars were flickering out,
I dropped the berry in a stream
And caught a little silver trout.

When I had laid it on the floor
I went to blow the fire aflame,
But something rustled on the floor,
And some one called me by my name;
It had become a glimmering girl
With apple blossom in her hair
Who called me by my name and ran
And faded through the brightening air.

Though I am old with wandering
Through hollow lands and hilly lands,
I will find out where she has gone,
And kiss her lips and take her hands;
And walk among long dappled grass,
And pluck till time and times are done,
The silver apples of the moon,
The golden apples of the sun.

W. B. Yeats

Moonlit Apples

At the top of the house the apples are laid in rows,
And the skylight lets the moonlight in, and those
Apples are deep-sea apples of green. There goes
    A cloud on the moon in the autumn night.

A mouse in the wainscot scratches, and scratches,
    and then
There is no sound at the top of the house of men
Or mice; and the cloud is blown, and the moon again
    Dapples the apples with deep-sea light.

They are lying in rows there, under the gloomy beams;
On the sagging floor; they gather the silver streams
Out of the moon, those moonlit apples of dreams,
    And quiet is the steep stair under.

In the corridors under there is nothing but sleep.
And stiller than ever on orchard boughs they keep
Tryst with the moon, and deep is the silence, deep
    On the moon-washed apples of wonder.

John Drinkwater

To Autumn

Season of mists and mellow fruitfulness!
    Close bosom-friend of the maturing sun;
Conspiring with him how to load and bless
    With fruit the vines that round the thatch-eaves run;
To bend with apples the moss'd cottage-trees,
    And fill all fruit with ripeness to the core;
        To swell the gourd, and plump the hazel shells
    With a sweet kernel; to set budding more,
And still more, later flowers for the bees,
Until they think warm days will never cease,
    For Summer has o'er-brimm'd their clammy cells.

Who hath not seen thee oft amid thy store?
    Sometimes whoever seeks abroad may find
Thee sitting careless on a granary floor,
    Thy hair soft-lifted by the winnowing wind;
Or on a half-reap'd furrow sound asleep,
    Drowsed with the fumes of poppies, while thy hook
        Spares the next swath and all its twinèd flowers;
And sometimes like a gleaner thou dost keep
    Steady thy laden head across a brook;
    Or by a cider-press, with patient look,
        Thou watchest the last oozings, hours by hours.

Where are the songs of Spring? Ay, where are they?
   Think not of them, thou hast thy music too,
While barrèd clouds bloom the soft-dying day,
   And touch the stubble-plains with rosy hue;
Then in a wailful choir the small gnats mourn
   Among the river sallows, borne aloft
      Or sinking as the light wind lives or dies;
And full-grown lambs loud bleat from hilly bourn;
   Hedge-crickets sing; and now with treble soft
   The redbreast whistles from a garden-croft,
      And gathering swallows twitter in the skies.

John Keats

Autumn Fires

In the other gardens
        And all up the vale,
From the autumn bonfires
        See the smoke trail!

Pleasant summer over
        And all the summer flowers,
The red fire blazes,
        The grey smoke towers.

Sing a song of seasons!
        Something bright in all!
Flowers in the summer,
        Fires in the fall!

Robert Louis Stevenson

The Garden in September

Now thin mists temper the slow-ripening beams
Of the September sun: his golden gleams
On gaudy flowers shine, that prank the rows
Of high-grown hollyhocks, and all tall shows
That Autumn flaunteth in his bushy bowers;
Where tomtits, hanging from the drooping heads
Of giant sunflowers, peck the nutty seeds;
And in the feather aster bees on wing
Seize and set free the honied flowers,
Till thousand stars leap with their visiting:
While ever across the path mazily flit,
Unpiloted in the sun,
The dreamt butterflies
With dazzling colours powdered and soft glooms,
White, black and crimson stripes, and peacock eyes,
Or on chance flowers sit,
With idle effort plundering one by one
The nectaries of deepest-throated blooms.

With gentle flaws the western breeze
Into the garden saileth,
Scarce here and there stirring the single trees,
For his sharpness he vaileth:
So long a comrade of the bearded corn,
Now from the stubbles whence the shocks are borne,

O'er dewy lawns he turns to stray,
As mindful of the kisses and soft play
Wherewith he enamoured the light-hearted May,
Ere he deserted her;
Lover of fragrance, and too late repents;
Nor more of heavy hyacinth now may drink,
Nor spicy pink,
Not summer's rose, nor garnered lavender,
But the few lingering scents
Of streakèd pea, and gillyflower, and stocks
Of courtly purple, and aromatic phlox.

   And at all times to hear are drowsy tones
Of dizzy flies, and humming drones,
With sudden flap of pigeon wings in the sky,
Or the wild cry
Of thirsty rooks, that scour ascare
The distant blue, to watering as they fare
With creaking pinions or – on business bent,
If aught their ancient polity displease, –
Come gathering to their colony, and there
Settling in ragged parliament,
Some stormy council hold in the high trees.

Robert Bridges

Remember, Remember

It didn't matter that the night was cold
or that our toes were numb in our boots
It didn't matter that the first frost
had crept across the grass like silvered dust
We stood together close to where the bonfire
threw flames that seemed to try to reach the moon
As fireworks scattered myriad dazzling stars into the night
the long and dancing shadows hid embarrassment
and rosy cheeks
As you said
You liked me
And in the crowd we stood a bit closer
and it didn't matter that the night was cold
or that our toes were numb in our boots
because you reached out and held my hand
and the world was never more warm

Dawn McLachlan

Pleasant Scents

The kitchen just before lunch on Christmas Day...
Salty spray when waves crash on rocks in the bay...
In school, when you model with clammy damp clay...
> *Pleasant scents*
> *that stay with you*
> *forever.*

The attic's dry air after days of June heat...
A shower of spring rain that refreshes the street...
An orange you peel: the tang sharp, yet so sweet...
> *Pleasant scents*
> *that stay with you*
> *forever.*

The Bonfire Night smoke as it drifts in the dark...
Air lemony-clean on the Island of Sark...
Mint in the back garden... and mud in the park...
> *Pleasant scents*
> *that stay with you*
> *forever.*

Wes Magee

Sonnet Moon

Moon plays Mozart on Spring evenings
Feather-soft notes
Tap at my window
Stirring my soul
Calming my mind

Moon sings the blues on Summer nights
Slow mellow tones
Creep through my window
Lull me to slumber
Till morning

Moon reads Kipling on crisp Autumn nights
Whispers of roads forgotten
But alive still
Brush at my window
Hush me to sleep

Moon reads Shakespeare on Winter eves
Sonnets of love
Enduring passion
Pirouette at my window and
Capture my heart.

Debra Bertulis

On the First Frost of Winter

The days have become shorter,
but magical nights full of lights are longer,

and the sweet spices of the mulled wine
your neighbours are making fills the air.

You are older now by a whole year,
and you let the ice do its work of melting away pain.

You watch your breath mist against the window,
and gently write the words, 'I was here.'

Nikita Gill

Raised in Rhyme

I was born out in the wilderness, beneath a sky so cold
With a sword for my deliverance and no human hand to
    hold,
But the constellations rocked me in the rhythm of all time
And I stood up, glad to be alive, raised up in a rhyme.

I tried my feet upon the ground, but I couldn't find a way.
I wandered in confusion, never knowing night from day.
But a woodlark and nightingale sang out to show the line
That lies between the dark and light, and raised me up in
    rhyme.

I waited at the mountain, I waited by the sea;
Never was there anybody waiting there for me,
But the waves and trees and flowers swayed and shone
    with such a shine
That my heart just kept on dancing, cos I was raised in
    rhyme.

The tangled green of jungle, the ocean's deepest blue
The tardigrade, the python and the bouncing kangaroo
All of life's a lyric in a song of the sublime,
Written in one language and raised up in a rhyme.

I lift my head to sunset, feel its warmth upon my face
I know that when I'm gone from here that I won't leave a trace,
But I am filled with poems, moon and stars in every line
I'm a baby of the universe cos I was raised in rhyme.

Nicola Davies

A Good Book

Part of the pleasure is roaming the bookshelves.
   Part of the pleasure is reading the blurbs.
Part of the pleasure is judging the covers.
   Part of the pleasure is mouthing the words.

Part of the pleasure is sniffing the paper.
   Part of the pleasure is skimming the start.
Part of the pleasure is testing the title
   to see if it speaks to your head and your heart.

Part of the pleasure is flicking for pictures.
   Part of the pleasure's the lines of the font.
Part of the pleasure is asking the questions:
   What do I feel like? What do I want?

Part of the pleasure is jumping round genres,
   trying on worlds like a new pair of shoes.
Part of the pleasure's unveiling your treasure –
   so tell me, oh reader, which book did you choose?

Rachel Piercey

Poetry

The softness of the lemon in a primrose
the nodding of bowed bluebell from a bee
the silence in the gaps of a bird's song
the library of the creatures in a tree
the plumping of a plum in the sunshine
the crazy path an ant left in the grass
the fleeting blue-pink-orange evening
the moment when the sky darks for the stars
the goosebumps that run from haunting music
the bounce of the branch as bird flies free
the smell of the earth rise after rainfall
the little moments that make life's poetry

Liz Brownlee

This Poem . . .

This poem is dangerous: it should not be left
Within the reach of children, or even of adults
Who might swallow it whole, with possibly
Undesirable side-effects. If you come across
An unattended, unidentified poem
In a public place, do not attempt to tackle it
Yourself. Send it (preferably, in a sealed container)
To the nearest centre of learning, where it will be rendered
Harmless, by experts. Even the simplest poem
May destroy your immunity to human emotions.
All poems must carry a Government warning. Words
Can seriously affect your heart.

Elma Mitchell

Between the Covers

I sit soft on the sofa
with snow whipping my eyes,
with chill rock against my cheek.

Wolves howl,
but their tiny voices
vanish in the storm.

I need shelter,
to get under cover,
find a cave.

My cloak so thin,
my boots full of slush,
my eyes sting and my cheeks crackle.

I get up,
make a cup of tea,
look out the kitchen window at the summer.

A blackbird hops on the fence,
eying worms,
singing his snatch of sunlit song,

and then –
back to the sofa,
back to the mountain,
back to the winter,
back to the book.

A. F. Harrold

The Lake Isle of Innisfree

I will arise and go now, and go to Innisfree,
And a small cabin build there, of clay and wattles made:
Nine bean-rows will I have there, a hive for the honey-bee,
And live alone in the bee-loud glade.

And I shall have some peace there, for peace comes
    dropping slow,
Dropping from the veils of the morning to where the
    cricket sings;
There midnight's all a glimmer, and noon a purple glow,
And evening full of the linnet's wings.

I will arise and go now, for always night and day
I hear lake water lapping with low sounds by the shore;
While I stand on the roadway, or on the pavements grey,
I hear it in the deep heart's core.

W. B. Yeats

The Promenade of Whitley Bay

after W. B. Yeats

I will arise and go now, and go to Whitley Bay.
And check myself into a snug B&B:
with a Single Room, a Shared Bathroom,
(and no Sea View).

A weary wooden desk I will have there,
for my half-filled notebook and my rollerball pens.
To live alone and scrawl my thoughts
beside the windswept Promenade.

And I shall have some peace there.
Hands wedged deeply in pockets,
tartan scarf and Dr Martens.
A gusty hike from Tynemouth
before the Rendezvous
for chocolate and coffee.

I'll let the sea breeze sting my cheeks
on the rocks of St Mary's Island.
Before purple ink runs riot when I tuck myself away.
The corner table of a toasty tavern:
silent and invisible.
And when my tide is at its lowest,
I'll swan-dive into dog-eared books.

I will arise and go now, for always night and day,
I hear karaoke from The Victoria;
Smell crispy batter from the Arcade;
Sigh with satisfaction, as my notebook slaps shut.
Feel that windswept Promenade
deep in my gut.

Matt Abbott

Pangur Bán

I and Pangur Bán, my cat,
'Tis a like task we are at;
Hunting mice is his delight,
Hunting words I sit all night.

Better far than praise of men
'Tis to sit with book and pen;
Pangur bears me no ill-will,
He too plies his simple skill.

'Tis a merry thing to see
At our tasks how glad are we,
When at home we sit and find
Entertainment to our mind.

Oftentimes a mouse will stray
In the hero Pangur's way;
Oftentimes my keen thought set
Takes a meaning in its net.

'Gainst the wall he sets his eye
Full and fierce and sharp and sly;
'Gainst the wall of knowledge I
All my little wisdom try.

When a mouse darts from its den,
O how glad is Pangur then!
O what gladness do I prove
When I solve the doubts I love!

So in peace our tasks we ply,
Pangur Bán, my cat, and I;
In our arts we find our bliss,
I have mine and he has his.

Practice every day has made
Pangur perfect in his trade;
I get wisdom day and night
Turning darkness into light.

Anon., translated by Robin Flower

Refuge

While shout and tingle ebb from ringing ears,
flush fades from angry faces, and the house
catches itself, beginning to breathe deep
and take stock of the damage, she creeps up
the ladder in the library, fingers deft
at cataloguing spines by touch, and finds
a friend in the thick darkness, quiet and still.

Swathed rich in moth-holed softness, dust and time,
she reads for nourishment words known like her own skin:
feasts shared and varied, lazy by the sea;
discoveries; sharp triumph against long odds;
wit cracking dullness open to reveal
a broken cipher or a golden key –
a press of hands, a stirring of new gods.

Imogen Russell Williams

Rainy Day at the Caravan

The rain's drumming hard on the rooftop,
Our hiking boots damp by the door –
The windows are steamy; the weather's set in –
We're not going out, that's for sure.

I'm Laura in her covered wagon,
Or maybe a hedge-living mouse –
I'm Bilbo who's finally back at *Bag End*
and wrapped in the hug of his house.

Mum's clattering cups in the kitchen –
She's making hot chocolates all round,
The kettle is whistling shrill on the hob –
It's oddly a comforting sound.

I'm Heidi tucked up in her hayloft,
Mr Fox in his warm cosy den,
On board with the Gyptians like Lyra and Pan
as we sail across river and fen.

Dad's adding a piece to the jigsaw,
while Luna curls up and starts snoring –
I help with a bit that he couldn't make fit,
and somehow it doesn't seem boring.

I'm a Borrower under the floorboards,
Or Tottie now Marchpane has gone –
I've woken up here at *The Burrow*,
as a guest of the Weasleys and Ron.

Tomorrow the forecast looks better,
The sun will be out, as will we –
But for now, I'm just snug in a story,
and this time – the character's me.

Sarah Ziman

Can you name the books this poem references?

Little House on the Prairie – Laura Ingalls Wilder
The *Brambly Hedge* series – Jill Barklem
The Hobbit – J.R.R. Tolkien
Heidi – Johanna Spyri
Fantastic Mr. Fox – Roald Dahl
Northern Lights – Philip Pullman
The Borrowers – Mary Norton
The Dolls' House – Rumer Godden
Harry Potter and the Chamber of Secrets – J.K. Rowling

Mr McGuire

Mr McGuire, blind as a bat,
Had a rabbit, a weasel, a dog and a cat.
He stroked them all as he sat by the fire,
Some days they felt smooth
And some days like wire.
With a bark, a hiss, a squeak and miaow
They demanded his attention
And all got it somehow.
Old Mr McGuire, he loved them all–
'To me you are one creature,
You're from the same sack.
God brought you here
And he'll take you back.
You may think you are all different
But, heavens above,
You are all loved with one single love.'

Brian Patten

Love

Down the road
And through the gate,
Leave behind
The things I hate:
Traffic, noise,
Stress and fuss.
I'm home first –
There's only us.

We cuddle up
On the chair,
I run my fingers
Through your ... fur
You gaze at me
With loving eyes.
Your nose is wet –
That's no surprise.

Then, perhaps,
An evening walk –
You *always* listen
When I talk.
I love my family,
Of course I do –
But most of all,
Dog, I love you.

J. H. Rice

Happy

dog on a long walk

dog in the sea

dog in a basket

me on the settee

dog with a biscuit

dog on my knee

my happy dog

and his happy me!

Sue Cowling

The Shape of a Good Greyhound

A head like a snake,
a neck like a drake.
A back like a beam,
a belly like a bream.
A foot like a cat,
a tail like a rat.

Anon.

from The Winter Morning Walk

Forth goes the woodman, leaving unconcern'd
The cheerful haunts of man: to wield the axe
And drive the wedge, in yonder forest drear,
From morn to eve his solitary task.
Shaggy, and lean, and shrewd, with pointed ears
And tail cropp'd short, half-lurcher and half-cur,
His dog attends him. Close behind his heel
Now creeps he slow; and now, with many a frisk
Wide -scamp'ring, snatches up the drifted snow
With iv'ry teeth, or ploughs it with his snout;
Then shakes his powder'd coat, and barks for joy.

William Cowper

Dog

You little friend, your nose is ready; you sniff,
Asking for that expected walk,
(Your nostrils full of the happy rabbit-whiff)
And almost talk.

And so the moment becomes a moving force;
Coats glide down from their pegs in the humble dark;
The sticks grow live to the stride of their vagrant course.
You scamper the stairs,
Your body informed with the scent and the track and
    the mark
Of stoats and weasels, moles and badgers and hares.

We are going OUT. You know the pitch of the word,
Probing the tone of thought as it comes through fog
And reaches by devious means (half-smelt, half-heard)
The four-legged brain of a walk-ecstatic dog.

Out in the garden your head is already low.
(Can you smell the rose? Ah, no.)
But your limbs can draw
Life from the earth through the touch of your padded paw.

Now, sending a little look to us behind,
Who follow slowly the track of your lovely play,
You carry our bodies forward away from mind
Into the light and fun of your useless day.

Thus, for your walk, we took ourselves, and went
Out by the hedge and the tree to the open ground.
You ran, in delightful strata of wafted scent,
Over the hill without seeing the view;
Beauty is smell upon primitive smell to you:
To you, as to us, it is distant and rarely found.

Home . . . and further joy will be surely there:
Supper waiting full of the taste of bone.
You throw up your nose again, and sniff, and stare
For the rapture known

Of the quick wild gorge of food and the still lie-down
While your people talk above you in the light
Of candles, and your dreams will merge and drown
Into the bed-delicious hours of night.

Harold Monro

The Now Dog

Tired of scrolling through dogs doing tricks on TikTok
Your undulating tummy catches my eye

Your heavy paw judders
on the bridge of your nose
and I wonder if you're dreaming of the thunder
we ran under
to beat the rain home
after our morning walk in the woods

I crawl from the sofa
to lie with you by the fire
And as I watch your belly rise and fall
I gently lay my arm over your heated fur
and for a moment you stir, slightly opening one eye
as your hot breath exhales a happy sigh
so does mine
and both of us smile

I slow my breath to sync with yours
I gently squeeze one of your paws
as our thoughts sink and wing towards dreams

Silence descends
and the last thing I hear
on that rainy afternoon in June
is the tick tock of the clock on the wall
and the washing machine's hum
the faint chatter of Mum
and me and you here
breathing as one

Mark Bird

How to Work like a Dog

After a big bark at the sauntering cats,
the chittering cheek of squirrels, shaking trees
that might be birds or badness yet unknown –

after the tasting of the air, wet-nosed
after the wee-graffiti down the road
('was here' 'was here' 'was here' 'was here' 'was here') –

after a huge eccentric oval run
powered by ears and tail, a dive, a roll
in something noxious, and a sullen bath –

then the great work of golden day begins.
Curl into bagel, stretch into baguette,
nestle in basket like a proving loaf,

and snore-breathe. Chase slow feasts of ideal prey
through dreams of twitch and whimper. Chase the sun
across the room, from rug to chair to knee.

Imogen Russell Williams

Judy's on the Case

If you're low or if you're down
Someone's calling you a clown
If your book's become unbound
Judy's on the case

When the day is running out
Your head is full of nagging doubt
And you want to scream and shout
Judy's on the case

The disappointment of a friend
A broken cup that will not mend
An uphill road that has no end
Judy's on the case

When Judy greets you she goes crazy
She says, *I love you – you amaze me*
Let's play a game
Come on, be quick
A woof, a hug, a big wet lick
You're the best, in all the land

Judy's got the case in hand

Roger Stevens

On ',,,;;pppppp'[[[[[[[[[[[;';
///////////////////////3,'

Upon returning to my desk,
having left it temporarily in search of biscuits,
I discovered my cat had written
another poem on my laptop.

It was called ',,,;;pppppp'[[[[[[[[[[[;';///////////////////////3,'
and while it constituted one of her more difficult pieces,
it was also the kind of poem
which rewarded repeat reading.

I was struck by its experimental structure,
the absence of line breaks;
indeed, not one single space
between any of the poem's 10,000 or so characters.

One of the work's central motifs –
'jjjjjjjjjjjjjjjjjjjjjjjjjjjjjjjjjjjjjjjkkkkkkkkkkkkkkkkkkkk' –
was, by turns, reassuring and unsettling,
while the symbolism of '###################'

hinted at our twenty-first century preoccupation with
   social media.
And yes, there were perhaps a few elements
which did not work: twelve whole pages
containing just the number 7 seemed a little excessive,

while her introduction of the character T
was not altogether convincing. But who could not be moved
by that devastating final line, its message of hope
   piercing our hearts like an arrow: 333333333333333,,,

Brian Bilston

The Queen

She is a queen.
She slinks
stealthily,
soft fur rippling
as she comes to sit on my lap.
She kneads it,
and nudges my hand
until I stroke her ears,
then her back.
She smells like outside
like fresh air
and frosty, starlit nights.
She rolls over
purring loudly
happily
joyfully
as I tickle her tummy,
then she pounces on my hand
shakes her head in disgust
saunters off to the other end of the sofa,
curls up and sighs.

Naomi Jones

Happiness Motor

she
  pours through the flap
    sits on the mat
      leaps on your lap
        and turns on
          her happiness motor

she
  hunts in lines
    washes in knots
      plays in circles
        and turns on
          her happiness motor

she
  blinks yellow
    yawns pink
      scratches red
        and turns off
          her happiness motor

she
  tiptoes in circles
    settles in a curl
      plays the piano
        and turns on
          her happiness motor

Mandy Coe

Applause

I gave my cat a six-minute standing ovation
For services rendered: hunting of very small game,

Pouncing about and sitting in cardboard boxes,
Three-legged washing and never knowing his name,

The jump on the knee, the nuzzle at night, the kneading
Of dough with his paws, the punch at the candle flame,

The yowling for food, the looking at everything otherwise,
Staring through it straight with a faraway aim.

I gave my cat a six-minute standing ovation.
Your cat's like that? I think you should do the same.

Kit Wright

from Jubilate Agno

For I will consider my cat Jeoffry.
For he is the servant of the living God, duly and daily
    serving him.
For at the first glance of the glory of God in the East
    he worships in his way.
For this is done by wreathing his body seven times round
    with elegant quickness.
For when he leaps up to catch the musk, which is the
    blessing of God upon his prayer.
For he rolls upon prank to work it in.
For having done duty and received blessing he begins to
    consider himself.
For this he performs in ten degrees.
For first he looks upon his fore-paws to see if they are clean.
For secondly he kicks up behind to clear away there.
For thirdly he works it upon stretch with the fore-paws
    extended.
For fourthly he sharpens his paws by wood.
For fifthly he washes himself.
For sixthly he rolls upon wash.
For seventhly he fleas himself, that he may not be
    interrupted upon the beat.
For eighthly he rubs himself against a post.
For ninthly he looks up for his instructions.

For tenthly he goes in quest of food.

For having consider'd God and himself he will consider his neighbour.

For if he meets another cat he will kiss her in kindness.

For when he takes his prey he plays with it to give it a chance.

For one mouse in seven escapes by his dallying.

For when his day's work is done his business more properly begins.

For he keeps the Lord's watch in the night against the adversary.

For he counteracts the powers of darkness by his electrical skin and glaring eyes.

For he counteracts the Devil, who is death, by brisking about the life.

For in his morning orisons he loves the sun and the sun loves him.

For he is of the tribe of Tiger.

For the Cherub Cat is a term of the Angel Tiger.

For he has the subtlety and hissing of a serpent, which in goodness he suppresses.

For he will not do destruction, if he is well-fed, neither will he spit without provocation.

For he purrs in thankfulness, when God tells him he's a good Cat.

For he is an instrument for the children to learn benevolence upon.

For every house is incompleat without him & a blessing is lacking in the Spirit.

For the Lord commanded Moses concerning the cats
    at the departure of the Children of Israel from Egypt.
For every family had one cat at least in the bag.
For the English cats are the best in Europe.
For he is the cleanest in the use of his fore-paws of any
    quadrupeds.
For the dexterity of his defence is an instance of the love
    of God to him exceedingly.
For he is the quickest to his mark of any creature.
For he is tenacious of his point.
For he is a mixture of gravity and waggery.
For he knows that God is his Saviour.
For there is nothing sweeter than his peace when at rest.
For there is nothing brisker than his life when in motion.
For he is of the Lord's poor and so indeed is he called
    by benevolence perpetually – Poor Jeoffry! poor
Jeoffry! the rat has bit thy throat.
For I bless the name of the Lord Jesus that Jeoffry is better.
For the divine spirit comes about his body to sustain it in
    compleat cat.
For his tongue is exceeding pure so that it has in purity
    what it wants in musick.
For he is docile and can learn certain things.
For he can set up with gravity which is patience upon
    approbation.
For he can fetch and carry, which is patience in
    employment.
For he can jump over a stick which is patience upon
    proof positive.

For he can spraggle upon waggle at the word of command.
For he can jump from an eminence into his master's bosom.
For he can catch the cork and toss it again.
For he is hated by the hypocrite and miser.
For the former is afraid of detection.
For the latter refuses the charge.
For he camels his back to bear the first motion of business.
For he is good to think on, if a man would express himself neatly.
For he made a great figure in Egypt for his signal services.
For he killed the Icneumon-rat very pernicious by land.
For his ears are so acute that they sting again.
For from this proceeds the passing quickness of his attention.
For by stroaking of him I have found out electricity.
For I perceived God's light about him both wax and fire.
For the Electrical fire is the spiritual substance, which God sends from heaven to sustain the bodies both of man and beast.
For God has blessed him in the variety of his movements.
For, tho he cannot fly, he is an excellent clamberer.
For his motions upon the face of the earth are more than any other quadrupeds.
For he can tread to all the measures upon the musick.
For he can swim for life.
For he can creep.

Christopher Smart

and a tree

Commissioned by the Poetry Society
for the 2022 Trafalgar Square Christmas Tree

and a tree is a promise
safe-kept by a seed,
and a tree is a dance
that is swung by the breeze,

and a tree is an engine
spinning only on air
and water and light;
nothing lost, nothing spare,

and a tree is a king
who is topped with a crown,
(and a tree never once
loses touch with the ground)

and a tree is a home
with numberless doors,
and a tree is a world
for an ant to explore,

and a tree is a gift
(for a tree is a lung)
and a tree is a song

that is whispered and sung
by the bees and the birds,
and in rustles and creaks,
yes, a tree is a song
that is sung without words,

and a tree is a lesson
in the meaning of roots,
and how out of the mud
swell the sweetest of fruits,

and a tree is a story
of hope and repair,
or perhaps more a question;
a wish or a prayer,
for a tree (plus a tree)
shows us how we might share,

and when we should grow
and when we should sleep
and what we could lose

and what we must keep.

Kate Wakeling

The Copper Beech at Fagervik

For Ola

As hard as I try, my arms cannot stretch
round your thick, wrinkly trunk that is carefully etched
with a century's carvings and towers above
any minuscule human. And boy, do I love

all the catkins that dangle like tassels from stalks,
and crunch underfoot whenever I walk
underneath you or push myself off for a swing.
How did nature create such a marvellous thing?

And when autumn arrives, you transform and you glow
a bright copper that waves through the windows below,
and your zigzagging branches assure me that I'm
part of nature, like you. I can patiently climb

until I'm giant too. So, I stretch and I reach ...
And you whisper, *'Take heed of this elderly beech –
look how quickly you grow! Now, whatever you do,
make sure you take time to savour the view.'*

Laura Mucha

Pied Beauty

Glory be to God for dappled things –
  For skies of couple-colour as a brinded cow;
    For rose-moles all in stipple upon trout that swim;
Fresh-firecoal chestnut-falls; finches' wings;
  Landscape plotted and pierced – fold, fallow, and
    plough;
    And áll trádes, their gear and tackle and trim.

All things counter, original, spare, strange;
  Whatever is fickle, freckled (who knows how?)
  With swift, slow; sweet, sour; adazzle, dim;
He fathers-forth whose beauty is past change:
    Praise him.

Gerard Manley Hopkins

The Glory

The glory of the beauty of the morning, –
The cuckoo crying over the untouched dew;
The blackbird that has found it, and the dove
That tempts me on to something sweeter than love;
White clouds ranged even and fair as new-mown hay;
The heat, the stir, the sublime vacancy
Of sky and meadow and forest and my own heart: –
The glory invites me, yet it leaves me scorning
All I can ever do, all I can be,
Beside the lovely of motion, shape, and hue,
The happiness I fancy fit to dwell
In beauty's presence. Shall I now this day
Begin to seek as far as heaven, as hell,
Wisdom or strength to match this beauty, start
And tread the pale dust pitted with small dark drops,
In hope to find whatever it is I seek,
Hearkening to short-lived happy-seeming things
That we know naught of, in the hazel copse?
Or must I be content with discontent
As larks and swallows are perhaps with wings?
And shall I ask at the day's end once more
What beauty is, and what I can have meant
By happiness? And shall I let all go,
Glad, weary, or both? Or shall I perhaps know
That I was happy oft and oft before,
Awhile forgetting how I am fast pent,
How dreary-swift, with naught to travel to,
Is Time? I cannot bite the day to the core.

Edward Thomas

from To General Hamley

Our birches yellowing and from each
    The light leaf falling fast,
While squirrels from our fiery beech
    Were bearing off the mast,
You came, and look'd and loved the view
    Long-known and loved by me,
Green Sussex fading into blue
    With one gray glimpse of sea.

Alfred, Lord Tennyson

On the Sussex Downs

Over the downs there were birds flying,
   Far off glittered the sea,
And toward the north the weald of Sussex
   Lay like a kingdom under me.

I was happier than the larks
   That nest on the downs and sing to the sky –
Over the downs the birds flying
   Were not so happy as I.

It was not you, though you were near,
   Though you were good to hear and see,
It was not earth, it was not heaven,
   It was myself that sang in me.

Sara Teasdale

Who Goes Where?

The rook to her branch in the swaying ash tree,
The gull to her sandbank in the wind's lee.

The frog to her sanctuary in the pond's mud,
The otter to her holt above the stream's flood.

The squirrel to her drey all lined with leaves
The mouse to her burrow hidden under the sheaves.

The owl to her perch on the barn's highest beam,
The louse to her hideout inside a seam.

And where will I go to find peace and rest?
To the arms of the one who loves me the best!

Nicola Davies

Crowds of Clouds

I have spent days
lying on my back
staring up at the high clouds drifting by.

Spotting shapes.
Naming maps.
Watching as the wind tugs at different speeds
mutating
the seeds
of imagination.

So big and fluffy
and wispy and gone.

Sometimes
I poke my arms out,
twist my legs in odd ways,
push up my tummy,
contort my body,
pull a face,
try to be
as interestingly-shaped
as those huge silent drifters.

They've given me joy,
so much joy,
I want to give them something back.

If they look down
I hope they see the odd-shaped me and smile,
even if they can't tell
exactly what I am,
I want to be a cloud-pleaser,
giving imagination to whole crowds of clouds
off to let out their rain
elsewhere.

A. F. Harrold

Careless Rambles

I love to wander at my idle will
   In summer's luscious prime about the fields,
To kneel, when thirsty, at the little rill
   And sip the draught its pebbly bottom yields,
And where the maple bush its fountain shields
   To lie and rest a sultry hour away,
Cropping the swelling peascod from the land,
   Or mid the sheltering woodland -walks to stray
Where oaks for aye o'er their old shadows stand
'Neath whose dark foliage with a welcome hand
   I pluck the luscious strawberry, ripe and red
As Beauty's lips – and in my fancy's dreams
   As 'mid the velvet moss I musing tread
Feel life as lovely as her picture seems.

John Clare

Two Haikus

Each day I wake to
lace curtains at my window –
why, thank you spider!

Car windscreen wipers:
metronomes for the music
of the morning rain

Graham Denton

On the First Leaves of Autumn

Between hot chocolate and pumpkin spice,
mellow warmth and misty mornings,

the gold of your mother shines
alongside your father's glowing smile.

Your grandmother bakes buttery cookies,
while your grandfather rakes the amber-orange garden.

In a season where everything leaves,
you learn the fine art of loving and letting go.

Nikita Gill

Out at Sea

My boots crunch
on the shiny pebbles
that line the shore.
Waves lap like kittens' tongues
as the seaweed sets aflame.
Last night's grubby dishes
are piled between the deckchairs.
Beneath every grain of sand
is an urgent unread email.

I clamber into my one-man boat.
Set sail.

In my rucksack, I have everything
I could ever possibly need.
The latest issue
of my favourite mag.
A multipack of bourbons.

Steaming flask of Yorkshire Tea.
Tatty tartan blanket.
Framed photo of wife and son.
Size 4 football.

As I bob towards the horizon,
the beach becomes a blur.

There are mermaids who serenade
with Arctic Monkeys.
And the sea spray smells precisely
of golden buttery toast.

As I weave across the water,
the beach is now invisible.

My blanket becomes the radiators
from Nan's flat.
I'm flicking between articles
on Argentinian football.
I dunk a bourbon in my tea.
Readjust my bottom.
Give a smiling nod to the dolphins
who dance and leap around me.

The rhythm of the ocean
rocks me like a newborn.
A rainbow slowly emerges
as I stretch out and yawn.

I have hours
and hours
till I need to sail on back.
The water glistens,
turquoise and silver
as the mermaids
sing lullabies.

Matt Abbott

The Hut by the Sea

Here is my hut beside the hilly sea,
    A sweet, small resting-place, so soft and warm,
Though framed by desolate immensity,
    And rocked within the arms of every storm.

Each home where love abides is even so,
    A steadfast joy beneath a changing sky;
And all the storms of life that round it blow
    Are but its cradle and its lullaby.

Ethelwyn Wetherald

The Little Hill

This is the hill, ringed by the misty shire –
The mossy, southern hill,
The little hill where larches climb so high.
Among the stars aslant
They chant;
Along the purple lower slopes they lie
In lazy golden smoke, more faint, more still
Than the pale woodsmoke of the cottage fire.
Here some calm Presence takes me by the hand
And all my heart is lifted by the chant
Of them that lean aslant
In golden smoke, and sing, and softly bend:
And out from every larch-bole steals a friend.

Mary Webb

Something Told the Wild Geese

Something told the wild geese
   It was time to go.
Though the fields lay golden
   Something whispered,—'Snow.'
Leaves were green and stirring,
   Berries, luster-glossed,
But beneath warm feathers
   Something cautioned,—'Frost.'
All the sagging orchards
   Steamed with amber spice,
But each wild breast stiffened
   At remembered ice.
Something told the wild geese
   It was time to fly,—
Summer sun was on their wings,
   Winter in their cry.

Rachel Field

Pleasant Sounds

The rustling of leaves under the feet in woods and under hedges;
The crumping of cat-ice and snow down wood-rides, narrow lanes, and every street causeway;
Rustling through a wood or rather rushing, while the wind halloos in the oak-top like thunder;
The rustle of birds' wings startled from their nests or flying unseen into the bushes;
The whizzing of larger birds overhead in a wood, such as crows, puddocks, buzzards;
The trample of robins and woodlarks on the brown leaves, and the patter of squirrels on the green moss;
The fall of an acorn on the ground, the pattering of nuts on the hazel branches as they fall from ripeness;
The flirt of the groundlark's wing from the stubbles – how sweet such pictures on dewy mornings, when the dew flashes from its brown feathers!

John Clare

The Lane

Some day, I think, there will be people enough
In Froxfield to pick all the blackberries
Out of the hedges of Green Lane, the straight
Broad lane where now September hides herself
In bracken and blackberry, harebell and dwarf gorse.
Today, where yesterday a hundred sheep
Were nibbling, halcyon bells shake to the sway
Of waters that no vessel ever sailed ...
It is a kind of spring: the chaffinch tries
His song. For heat it is like summer too.
This might be winter's quiet. While the glint
Of hollies dark in the swollen hedges lasts –
One mile – and those bells ring, little I know
Or heed if time be still the same, until
The lane ends and once more all is the same.

Edward Thomas

Some Other Names for Rain

I call you the eyelash rinser
and windowpane racer.

I call you cloud soup.

I call you the tongue tickler,
sock seeper,
hair hassler
and ankle surpriser
(when paired with a passing car).

I call you sky spittle.

I call you leaf polisher.

I call you the pavement drummer
and umbrella summoner.

I call you a brigade of micro water bombs
having a skirmish with the lawn.

I call you the puddle artist
who will only draw circles.

I call you a sprinkle of ocean,
far from home.

Kate Wakeling

Tent

In my tent
The light is orange.
And I sit here
Still
As if I'm set in jelly.

It's magic here
In this gold space
Where a minute stretches on . . .
    and on . . . and on . . .

Jan Dean

Trips to the Seaside

The door slams behind us
and eternity waits in front.
A trip to the tip of the country.
A day to explore and escape.

Get your cozzy on,
take a deep breath,
and leave the land behind you . . .

Above head, the squawking
is warning on the breeze:
beware
any chips left unguarded!
The seagulls' choir:
it echoes and soothes.
S w o o p i n g
from the candy-floss sky.

The salty aroma
is thick and persistent:
from sea air
to sprinkles on chips.
It merges with sun cream
and sploshes of vinegar.
Wedged up our nostrils
till bedtime.

The sunlight is skipping
on dark, distant waves
and fighting its way
through clouds.
Fishing boats crawl
along the blurry horizon.
And swimsuits glisten
as they cling to wet skin.

Look! A shaggy dog
chasing a crimson ball.
Making ruins out of sandcastles
and panting in the sunshine.
Let's write our names by its footprints.
Introduce ourselves
to the starfish.

And the water
that's rushing
along pebbles,
towards toes:
inviting,
enthralling,
and frothy,
and fast.

And as we get closer
there's no turning back:
it races, outpaces,
and captures our ankles!

No water
has ever
been *colder*
than this.
No water
as cruel
or as
quick.

Jumpers for goalposts.
Giggles and singalongs.
Handstands
on harbour walls.
Books devoured in one.

Pockets crammed with delicate shells
or coins for arcades.
A day here
is as glorious
as *any*.

And it's a proven fact:
chips dipped in ketchup
and eaten from the paper
taste better
than anywhere else.

These doughnuts: exquisite.
These milkshakes: a triumph.
They soften the blow
of the sun
sinking
low . . .

      Oh,
           no!
                It's
                    time
                        to
                            go.

Matt Abbott

Thank you:

To the poets – thank you so much for letting me use your poems in this collection – so much warmth, comfort and peace.

To Nick de Somogyi – I am always so very grateful for your suggestions and input.

And huge thanks to the MCB team – Louisa Cusworth, Amy Boxshall, Tracey Ridgewell, Rachel Vale, Farzana Adlington, Anna Read and Sarah Ramsey.

Index of First Lines

A head like a snake 139
After a big bark at the sauntering cats 144
and a tree is a promise 155
And so I write 29
and we will open all the doors 10
As hard as I try, my arms cannot stretch 157
As she let the stillness settle 74
as the butterfly floats in the light-laden air 28
As the rain thunders 52
At day's end I remember 2
At the top of the house the apples are laid in rows 112
Between hot chocolate and pumpkin spice 167
Brand-new elephants roamed through the jungles 24
Bring me the sail of your breath 23
Car windscreen wipers 166
Close the door and turn the key 30
Come when the nights are bright with stars 71
Cosy is . . . 46
Cosy is comfort and cosy is snug 39
Courage is the price that Life exacts for granting peace 99
dog on a long walk 138
Down the road 137
Each day I wake to 166
Embers swirling, twirling, whirling 104
Every day is a fresh beginning 93

Everything is on fire 91
First, take a rain shower and run through it 48
For I will consider my cat Jeoffry 151
Forth goes the woodman, leaving unconcern'd 140
Give me a hug 33
Give me the long, straight road before me 100
Give me the splendid silent sun 102
Give yourself a hug 31
Glory be to God for dappled things 158
Go placidly amid the noise and haste 95
Gran pulls out yellow wool 55
Heading west, the names cwtch round 67
Her pockets are never empty 64
Here is my hut beside the hilly sea 170
House 38
I am the footsteps in the hall 78
I and Pangur Bán, my cat 131
I ask, and from the depths 37
I call you the eyelash rinser 175
I don't care if the winter comes 20
I felt wonder 25
I gave my cat a six-minute standing ovation 150
I have spent days 163
I heard there's a word in Bantu 43
I love to wander at my idle will 165
I saw dawn creep across the sky 1
I sit soft on the sofa 127

I was born out in the wilderness 122
I went out to the hazel wood 111
I will arise and go now, and go to Innisfree 128
I will arise and go now, and go to Whitley Bay 129
If you're low or if you're down 145
I'm tucked up 75
In my kitchen I have a little bottle of silence 63
In my tent 176
In the lanes there is still a negotiation with ice 7
In the other gardens 115
In the pitch-like night 101
It didn't matter that the night was cold 118
It gets darker later 70
It's not the bricks 35
It's warm by our fire 34
Joy at the silver birch fluffing its leaves 13
Let no one steal your dreams 12
Like a warning shot or a siren 89
Make new friends, but keep the old 18
May your smile be ever present 87
Moon plays Mozart on Spring evenings 120
Mr McGuire, blind as a bat 136
Mrs Everest is our headteacher 84
My boots crunch 168
My head is full of hurry 90
Not knowing where to look 108
Now thin mists temper the slow-ripening beams 116

Oh! I have slipped the surly bonds of earth 98
Oh, the comfort 15
Oh, warmth is sweeter after cold 47
Once we made a telephone 17
One voice 22
Open the window 68
Our birches yellowing and from each 160
Outside the sky is light with stars 72
Over the downs there were birds flying 161
Part of the pleasure is roaming the bookshelves 124
Rain dripping at the window 45
red flames flickering 103
Season of mists and mellow fruitfulness 113
She is a queen 148
She makes embroidery 58
she pours through the flap 149
She sits and knits 57
slapdash 79
Snug as a bug in a duvet-thick rug 32
Some day, I think, there will be people enough 174
Some friends are temporary 19
Something told the wild geese 172
Something worth losing 86
Sometimes we wear it like a scarf 88
Staring out of the window again 8
Such a sight I saw 26
Such a small word 40

The box tumbles open 60
The days have become shorter 121
The door slams behind us 177
The glory of the beauty of the morning 159
The hum of the city by night 77
The kitchen just before lunch on Christmas Day 119
The late September sunshine 107
The Music I like 65
The others have long since gone to bed 81
The rain's drumming hard on the rooftop 134
The rook to her branch in the swaying ash tree 162
The rustling of leaves under the feet in woods and under hedges 173
The softness of the lemon in a primrose 125
The waiter 51
the winds grip the trees 103
There is a band of dull gold in the west 73
There's a special light when it's nearly night 66
This is the hill, ringed by the misty shire 171
This poem is dangerous 126
Tired of scrolling through dogs doing tricks on TikTok 143
'Tis the human touch in this world that counts 21
To every thing there is a season 94
Today I think 105
Two church spires for ears 106
Under the green 85

Upon returning to my desk 146
We were walking in the woods 6
Well, I guess you've never heard 36
Wet denim clings like concrete 49
What is this life, if full of care 3
What is wellbeing, asks Sam 53
when I am 16
When things go wrong as they sometimes will 92
While shout and tingle ebb from ringing ears 133
wriggling niggles 103
You can watch red kites fly over Minchinhampton common 4
You little friend, your nose is ready 141
You need a strong core to excel at rock climbing 14
You're never first 82

Index of Authors and Translators

Abbott, Matt 60, 129, 168, 177
Anon. 131, 139
Awolola, Ruth 64, 86
Bertulis, Debra 120
Bilston, Brian 146
Bird, Mark 143
Bloom, Valerie 107
Bradman, Tony 34
Bridges, Robert 116
Brownlee, Liz 125
Camden, Steven 8
Carter, James 35
Clare, John 165, 173
Coe, Mandy 17, 149
Conlon, Dom 6, 70, 82
Cookson, Paul 12, 87
Coolidge, Susan 93
Corbett, Pie 4, 28, 108
Cowling, Sue 138
Cowper, William 140
Craik, Dinah Maria 15
Davies, Nicola 7, 30, 67, 122, 162
Davies, W. H. 3
Dawson, Sue Hardy 55, 88
de Roo, Elena 38, 77
Dean, Jan 2, 176
Denton, Graham 166
Dougherty, John 22

Drinkwater, John 112
Dunbar, Paul Laurence 71
Earhart, Amelia 99
Ehrmann, Max 95
Field, Rachel 1, 172
Flower, Robin 131
Free, Spencer Michael 21
Gill, Nikita 19, 91, 121, 167
Gittins, Chrissie 63, 84, 106
Harrold, A. F. 85, 101, 127, 163
Hopkins, Gerard Manley 158
Jones, Naomi 148
Joseph, Jenny 26
Keats, John 113
Lawrence, D. H. 73
MacRae, Lindsay 78
Magee, John Gillespie, Jr. 98
Magee, Wes 119
Mansfield, Katherine 72
McGough, Roger 13
McLachlan, Dawn 20, 118
McMillan, Ian 65
Mitchell, Elma 58, 126
Monro, Harold 141
Morgan, Michaela 45, 46
Mucha, Laura 16, 90, 157
Newberry, Jane 37
Newson, Karl 104
Nichols, Grace 31
Oliver, Rhiannon 32, 48, 66

Parry, Joseph 18
Patten, Brian 24, 136
Perry, Emma 74, 103
Piercey, Rachel 47, 75, 124
Rice, J. H. 137
Rice, John 68
Robertson, Shauna Darling 14, 43, 53, 81, 89
Runner, Olive 100
Seigal, Joshua 29
Shavick, Andrea 25
Sirdeshpande, Rashmi 52
Smart, Christopher 151
Stevens, Julie 23
Stevens, Roger 51, 145
Stevenson, Robert Louis 115
Teasdale, Sara 161
Tennyson, Alfred, Lord 160
Thomas, Edward 105, 159, 174
Toczek, Nick 36, 39
Wakeling, Kate 10, 155, 175
Warren, Celia 57
Webb, Mary 171
Wetherald, Ethelwyn 170
Whitman, Walt 102
Williams, Imogen Russell 49, 79, 133, 144
Wilson, Anna 40
Wright, Kit 150
Yeats, W. B. 111, 128
Zetter, Neal 33
Ziman, Sarah 134

Acknowledgements

Abbott, Matt: 'The Promenade of Whitley Bay', 'New Dad', 'Out at Sea', 'Trips to the Seaside', reproduced by kind permission of the author; **Awolola, Ruth:** 'Pockets', first published in *Rising Stars: New Young Voices in Poetry*, Otter-Barry Books, 2017, 'Small Things', first published in *PUSH Magazine*, The Writing Squad, 2021, © Ruth Awolola and reprinted by permission of the author; **Bertulis, Debra:** 'Sonnet Moon', previously published in 'Chasing Clouds', edited by Jonathan Humble, reproduced by kind permission of the author; **Bilston, Brian: On** ';..p'[[[[[[[[[[[[[[';//////////////////////////3,' from *Let Sleeping Cats Lie*, (Macmillan Children's books 2024) reprinted by Permission of the author; **Bird, Mark:** 'The Now Dog', reproduced by kind permission of the author; **Bloom, Valerie:** 'Autumn Gilt', © Valerie Bloom 2000 from *The River's a Singer* (Macmillan) reprinted by permission of Eddison Pearson Ltd on behalf of Valerie Bloom; **Bradman, Tony:** 'Winter', from *Smile, Please!* collection of poems by Tony Bradman, first published by Viking, 1986, Reproduced by permission of The Agency (London) Ltd © Tony Bradman, 1986; **Brownlee, Liz:** 'Poetry', reproduced by kind permission of the author; **Camden, Steven:** 'Gazelle', reproduced by kind permission of the author; **Carter, James:** 'Home', © James Carter, reproduced by kind permission of the author; **Coe, Mandy:** 'The Strawberry-Yogurt Smell of Words', first published in *Happy Poems: chosen by Roger McGough* (Macmillan Children's Books 2018), Happiness Motor reproduced by kind permission of the author; **Conlon, Dom:** 'Between You, Me and the Moon', and 'Quietly Remarkable', first published This Rock, That Rock (Troika) Dom Conlon / Viviane Schwarz, 'Wild Garlic', first published Welcome To Wild Town (Otter-Barry Books) Dom Conlon / A. F. Harrold /Korky Paul; **Cookson, Paul:** 'Let No-one Steal Your Dreams', 'May You Always', © Paul Cookson, reproduced by kind permission of the author; **Corbett, Pie:** '12 Good Things to do Where I Live', It Is Eternity Now', 'I Set Out to Seek the Truth', reproduced by kind permission of the author; **Cowling, Sue:** 'Happy', reproduced by kind permission of the author; **Darling Robertson, Shauna:** 'If We Have More Good Things, Do We Feel Better?', 'Things People Have Told Me in the Last Few Weeks', 'Sam Asks Alexa About Wellbeing', first published in: *You Are Not Alone* by Shauna Darling Robertson (Troika, 2023), 'A Reminder', 'At the Fireside', reproduced by kind permission of the author; **Davies, Nicola:** 'First Run of

Spring', 'Into the West', 'Raised in Rhyme', 'Twinkle Twinkle', 'Who Goes Where?', reproduced by kind permission of the author; **de Roo, Elena:** 'Lullaby', 'Home', reproduced by kind permission of the author; **Dean, Jan:** 'Tent', 'Three Good Things', © Jan Dean, reproduced by kind permission of the author; **Denton, Graham:** 'Car Windscreen Wipers', 'Each Day I Wake To', reproduced by kind permission of the author; **Dougherty, John:** 'One Voice', reproduced by kind permission of the author; **Gill, Nikita:** 'In 150 Characters or Less', 'On the First Frost of Winter', 'On the First Leaves of Autumn', 'Reminder on Friendship', from *These are the Words* by Nikita Gill © Nikita Gill, 2022, published by Macmillan Children's Books, reproduced by kind permission of David Higham Associates; **Gittins, Chrissie:** 'Mrs Everest', 'Suffolk Hare', 'The Little Bottle of Silence', reproduced by kind permission of the author; **Hardy Dawson, Sue:** 'Gran's Unknitting', 'Happiness', reproduced by kind permission of the author; **Harrold, A. F.:** 'Between the Covers', 'Crowds of Clouds', 'The Blink of a Mountain', 'The Train in the Night', © A. F. Harrold, reproduced by kind permission of the author; **Jones, Naomi:** 'The Queen', Printed by permission of United Agents (www.unitedagents.co.uk) on behalf of Naomi Jones; **Joseph, Jenny:** 'The Magic of the Brain', reproduced by permission of Johnson & Alcock Ltd; **Macrae, Lindsay:** 'I am the Lullaby', reproduced by kind permission of the author; **Magee, Wes:** 'Pleasant Scents', reproduced by kind permission of the author's estate; **McGough, Roger:** 'Joy at the Sound', Copyright © Roger McGough from *Good Enough to Eat* published by Puffin 2002 Reprinted by permission of Penguin Books Limited; **McLachlan, Dawn:** 'Laughter', 'Remember, Remember', reproduced by kind permission of the author; **McMillan, Ian:** 'The Music I Like', © Ian McMillan, reproduced by permission of UK Touring; **Mitchell, Elma:** 'This Poem...', 'Recreation', reproduced by kind permission of the author's estate; **Morgan, Michaela:** 'Cosy', 'What is Cosy?', reproduced by kind permission of the author; **Mucha, Laura:** 'Friend', 'My Head is Full of Hurry' from *Being Me: Poems about Thoughts, Worries and Feelings* by Liz Brownlee, Matt Goodfellow and Laura Mucha, Otter-Barry Books, 2021 and 'The Copper Beech at Fagervik', © Laura Mucha, reproduced by kind permission of David Higham Associates; **Newberry, Jane:** 'What Makes Home?', reproduced by kind permission of the author; **Newson, Karl:** 'Bonfire Stars', Printed by permission of United Agents (www.unitedagents.co.uk) on behalf of Karl Newson; **Nichols, Grace:** 'Give Yourself a Hug', Grace Nichols ©1994 Reproduced with permissions from Curtis Brown Group Ltd. on behalf of

Grace Nichols; **Oliver, Rhiannon:** 'A Recipe for Cosiness', 'Hug', 'Magic Hour at the Kitchen Disco', reproduced by kind permission of the author; **Patten, Brian:** 'Mr McGuire', 'Small Wonders', by Brian Patten. Copyright © Brian Patten. Reproduced by permission of the author c/o Rogers, Coleridge & White Ltd., 20 Powis Mews, London W11 1JN; **Perry, Emma:** 'The Power of Quiet', 'Three Autumn Haikus', Printed by permission of United Agents (www.unitedagents.co.uk) on behalf of Emma Perry; **Piercey, Rachel:** 'A Good Book', 'Blanket Song', 'Triolet in Praise of Contrast', reproduced by kind permission of the author; **Rice, J. H.:** 'Love', reproduced by kind permission of the author; **Rice, John:** 'Driving at Night with My Dad', reproduced by kind permission of the author; **Russell Williams, Imogen:** 'How to Work Like a Dog', 'Refuge', 'Nest', 'Hot Chocolate', ©Imogen Russell Williams 2023, reproduced by kind permission of the author; **Seigal, Joshua:** 'And So I Write', reproduced by kind permission of the author; **Shavick, Andrea:** 'I Felt Wonder', reproduced by kind permission of the author; **Sirdeshpande, Rashmi:** 'Hot Chocolate', reproduced by kind permission of the author; **Stevens, Julie:** 'See a Wish' First published by Flight of the Dragonfly Press, reproduced by kind permission of the author; **Stevens, Roger:** 'Hot Chocolate', 'Judy's on the Case', reproduced by kind permission of the author; **Toczek, Nick:** 'What Cosy Is', 'Hygge', reproduced by kind permission of the author; **Wakeling, Kate:** 'and a tree' was commissioned by The Poetry Society for the lighting-up ceremony of the Christmas Tree in Trafalgar Square, 2022 and is reprinted with permission from The Poetry Society and the author, 'Free' and 'Some Other Names for Rain', first published in *Cloud Soup* by Kate Wakeling (The Emma Press); **Warren, Celia:** 'Knit Two Together', © Celia Warren 2024, reproduced by kind permission of the author; **Wilson, Anna:** 'Cosy', reproduced by kind permission of the author; **Wright, Kit:** 'Applause', first published by Viking/Puffin, reproduced by kind permission of the author; **Zetter, Neal:** 'Hug', reproduced by kind permission of the author; **Ziman, Sarah:** 'Rainy Day at the Caravan', reproduced by kind permission of the author.

Every effort has been made to trace the copyright holders, but if any have been inadvertently overlooked, the publisher will be pleased to make the necessary arrangement at the first opportunity.